# Two Trashbags
### anecdotes of my father

by Jonathan Lane Yarboro

Two Trashbags: Anecdotes Of My Father
© Copyright 2014

All Rights Reserved.
No part of this book may be reproduced in any form without permission in writing from the author or publisher.

ISBN: 978-1-935256-44-1

**Ledge Press**
PO Box 1652
Boone, NC 28607
www.ledgepress.com
ledgepress@gmail.com

The style of *Two Trashbags* made it impossible to put down. It made me laugh when I probably shouldn't have and made me imagine smells I could never have dreamt. This book is a lot of fun.

    T.J. Fairchild, Business Owner,
    Commonplace Coffee, Indiana, PA


There is power in story. On multiple occasions in *Two Trashbags*, the author "drops bombs" and quickly moves on to the next antic. I found myself wanting more interpretation, but the storyline rolls on. But that's how life unfolds, isn't it? Spontaneous. Unpredictable. On-the-fly. Interrupted. Long after putting the book down, I still find myself pondering the implications of these adventures.

    Glen Massey, DMin,
    Pastor, Covenant Chapel, Kansas City, KS


These anecdotal stories provide the reader with a humorous foray through Jonathan Yarboro's father's life antics, related simply with a complex underpinning of chagrin at and perhaps grudging admiration for the outrageous perpetual adolescent who dared to confront life with brazen bravado and chutzpah."

    Korki Hanemann, Ph.D.
    Professor Emeritus, Campbell University

# **Praise for Two Trash Bags:**

If your relationship with your father is uncomplicated, angelic, or both, this book is not for you. However, if you have ever struggled with its meaning, whether your father loved you, or why humans seem to regularly question the relationship with their fathers, then read this book, immediately. It is clever, deeply funny, biting, and heartbreaking. However, in the end, it is a story of hope and reconciliation.

    Kurt D. Michael, Ph.D.,

    Professor, Psychologist, Father, Son


The story-telling in *Two Trashbags* is matter-of-fact and raw. There's no resolution. There's no condemnation. There's no "10 steps to being a better…whatever." There's simply a son recalling tales and adventures with his father that, while unique, colorful, and (at times) queasily entertaining, are powerfully real.

    Doc Hendley, Humanitarian

    Author, *Wine to Water*


*Two Trashbags* is one of those few stories that can make an endearing character out of a man who does reprehensible acts. While reading Jonathan Yarboro's biography of his father, I became acutely aware of my emotions and corresponding facial expressions drastically changing multiple times within each story – a smile creeping into a hearty laugh, a furrowed brow of concern, and back to huge smile.

    Catherine Marcum, Ph.D.

    Author of *Cyber Crime* and *Prison Sex*

In loving memory of my grandfather
Irvin Thomas Harden

*Thanks, Granddaddy, for teaching me
the importance and power of story.*

And in honor of my friend
Rick Trexler
who knew how important my father was to me
before I did.

# Contents

Prologue .................................................................. 3

Acknowledgements ................................................ 5

Introduction: Two Trash Bags ................................ 7

The First Trash Bag: His Antics ........................... 11
    Poker Face ........................................................ 13
    Commando ....................................................... 17
    The General ...................................................... 21
    Name Change ................................................... 27
    Backyard Buckshot ........................................... 31
    The Abyss .......................................................... 35
    Hussy Derby ...................................................... 39
    Kitty Kitty ......................................................... 43
    The Steed .......................................................... 49
    Catch Me If You Can ....................................... 53

Supplemental Interlude: His Ailments ................ 59

The Second Trash Bag: His Gross Antics ............ 67
    Put A Sock On It .............................................. 69
    Lay It Down ...................................................... 73
    Impacted ........................................................... 79
    Collateral Damage ............................................ 87

Conclusion: Dust and Bones ............................... 103

About The Author ................................................ 108

*Jack Lane Yarboro, Jr.*
*April 9, 1947 - January 9, 2013*

# Prologue

My father was a colorful man to say the least. Flashy. Imposing. Hairy. Generous. Prejudiced. Dyslexic. Uncouth. Wealthy. Bipolar. Fun. Foul-mouthed. Intelligent. Homeless. Embarrassing. Uneducated. Successful. Fat. Brazen. Addict. Poor. Handsome. Passionate. Driven. Undisciplined. Providing. Frightening. Strong. He was all of these during his lifetime.

On most levels, his was a tragic fall. But on another level, his fall was his salvation. Walking with him through it all was painful; but a few years before he died, I started to see his antics in a new light. I found that others, upon hearing his stories, found joy in their humor. And I suppose I started to see the humor as well, even if I did have to step away for a different perspective. I'm still not sure why I started writing them down, but at first the writing was a private exercise.

There are some stories yet untold: stories of his sneaking us into theme parks, of his clinging to sliding doors on hotel balconies out of his fear of heights, of his hustling people out of money at golf courses, of his shooting a possum with a .357 magnum on the front porch of our golf course home, and of his getting arrested for trying to get out of a grocery store with several pounds of steak hidden down his pants. Maybe one day I will tell them. But for now, they live only in my memory of him. These stories – the ones recorded here in this book – are the ones I penned before he died and a few I was able to write after he died. When he died I reflected on his life. I wondered for nearly a year whether I should be telling his stories in such a humorous and irreverent way, but I believe that to refrain from telling them would be to dishonor him. These are my dad's stories; and, though at times you will surely doubt it, they are true stories. I hope your experience in reading them gives you a hint of the train wreck I experienced in living them.

    Jonathan Yarboro
    Boone, NC
    January 2014

# Acknowledgements

Thank you to my feisty and supportive wife Felicia who wouldn't let me get away with not writing this. And thanks for loving Dad despite his many flaws.
*He loved you.*

Thanks to my sister, Anna Ramsey, for helping me get the facts straight.
*It was Eleuthra, after all. It's coming up!*

Thanks to my friend Evan Blackerby for showing me that just about anyone can quit talking and write a book.
*G.S.D.*

Thanks to my mom for loving me and protecting me through this craziness and so much more left untold.
*Keep holding your head high. You are a woman of grace.*

Thanks to the creative Kristin Espinosa for the idea and design of the cover. I love it when you take off and run with ideas.
*Fourteen is long gone.*

Thanks to Travis Suits, Mike Puckett, and Josh Littlejohn – three interns who helped me laugh through all this before Dad died.
*It's just a sagging skin suit!*

Thanks to Julie Winkles Osburn and Joanne King Cox, two friends who helped me fall in love with writing back in high school and were willing to take a look at this manuscript many years later and make it better.
*The Omnibus is coming!*

Thanks to Korki Hanemann who taught me that deliberate, beautiful writing is never finished.
*It might not be beautiful, but it's my Yawp!*

# Two Trashbags: An Introduction

Dad died in the wee hours of the morning while sleeping in his bed on January 9, 2013. He died in a house he had been living in for six months; and we – my wife, my mother, and my sister – were on our way there to collect his belongings. His living arrangements had been sketchy before, but this place added mystery to the mix. There had been no way to contact him other than on the cell phone of a woman who cleaned the house and cared for Dad on a part-time basis. He was unwilling to go to a facility that was on the up-and-up because they would not let him keep any of his money. He valued cigarettes and chocolate milk more than sanitation and ethics. Dad always had a strange way of looking at things.

When we pulled into the driveway, my sister looked at me and stated the obvious: "I'm nervous about going in there." We sat there in the driveway staring at the window in front of us, the window that until that morning had been my dad's window. The blinds were still closed. The two broken slats of those blinds still hung down like a symbol of what he had become. On the outside, everything looked just as it had ten days ago when we had last visited him. We took a deep breath, got out of the car, walked to the door, and rang the bell. Nothing. It turned out to be an anti-climactic arrival. No one ever came to the door. I walked around to the back of the house. Dad's wheelchair remained on the porch. I tried that door. Still nothing. My sister called the mysterious phone lady. No answer. She left a message. And together we waited. Hoping someone would show up. As we sat, we stared at that window…and those blinds.

To our surprise, the owner pulled up; and after the perfunctory condolences, he herded us through the front door into the quiet ghostliness of the house. No one was there. All the lights were off. We walked to his room, and the first thing that hit us was the bed. My sister and I just stopped in our tracks, frozen, looking at that bed. Other than the linens having been stripped off, the bare, plastic-covered mattress was the same one we had seen ten days earlier. Only then Dad had been sitting on it talking to us about memories of Big Cookies from Hardee's, stacking firewood on the back patio, the benefits of growing a beard, and scrubbing cat vomit off the garage floor…dreaming about how life would be better when he moved into a better facility and excited about the opportunity to see his grandchildren more often. This bed – the last place that had known his breath; the last place to have known the warmth of his big, hairy body; the last place he had occupied on this earth. For a few moments, we could do nothing but stand there and take it all in.

In the next hour, we filled trash bags – one for pictures and paperwork to take home and furrow through; a couple for trash to be discarded; several for clothes to be donated at a local charity; one for an old quilt that had been in our family for at least 25 years, the only thing still in his possession from our time as an intact family unit. We left the wheelchair and his nightstand for the house. Closing the door of my father's final abode on this earth, we placed the two trash bags in the trunk of the car. On the way home it struck me as terribly sad…that the entirety of his life left only two trash bags of things worth keeping around – pictures and a quilt.

Dad should have left a greater legacy than that. I remember when I was young, pulling up to a trailer park with him at Christmas, the car loaded with gifts wrapped in colorful paper and boxes of ham, corn, and beans – all gifts from Dad that he delivered to parents in each trailer so that they could be seen by their children as the providers for their own families. He was intentional in the way he explained that to me. Dad was a generous man, and he preferred to give in secret. Similarly, I remember his fondness for the Music Minister at my mom's church. Even though Dad wasn't a man of faith, he respected this man, especially his humility. Dad noticed that he wore the same suit week after week; so he acted. He drove down to the local men's store and gave the owner instructions to call that Minister of Music and inform him that he should come down to the store and pick out any two suits in the store, that an anonymous giver was going to cover all the costs. That man never found out who gave him those suits.

Like many men, as a husband and father, Dad desired to be a provider more than anything else. And for most of my adolescence, that's exactly what he was. My parents instilled in me a value system focused on giving rather than taking. Yet here we were, driving home with the remnants of his entire life occupying a mere two trash bags in the trunk of my car.

But as the days went by, I realized that he left more than that. He left the memories and the stories of how he shaped my life. These stories are his legacy. He liked to laugh. And from destroying public restrooms to taking extra communion wafers for snacks, he was wholly irreverent. The stories are a gift. And no two trash bags can contain them.

# The First Trashbag:
# His Antics

*Insanity runs in my family.
It practically gallops.*
— *Cary Grant*

# Poker Face

I don't know whether it was the beard, the voice, the size of the man, or his insurmountable self-confidence that served as the primary contributor to his convincing presence. Maybe it was a combination of several of these…or all of these…or something far more visceral. But there is no doubt about it – when my father spoke, people didn't just listen; they jumped.

Dad's office was an interesting place. Brightly colored flags waved along the road frontage like bikini-clad women beckoning perverted voyeurs to a carwash. Only they lined a lot full of manufactured homes. Not trailers, mind you. He kept a broken-down old block trailer on the lot just for the purpose of sarcastic mockery and setting the tone whenever someone walked into his office announcing he wanted to "buy a trailer". And not mobile homes either. "Mobile homes move around, and these homes have the wheels removed and replaced with brick underpinning." No, Dad declared emphatically that he sold *manufactured homes*. Just one more way he was convincing. Anyway, once potential customers pulled through the bright flags and past the impeccably manicured grass, they noticed the lined helicopter pad near the front door of his office – in the event that the president of the company decided to pop in for an impromptu visit.

Snapshots on bulletin boards filled the waiting area through the front door. The bulletin boards displayed pictures of him with satisfied customers, pictures of cranes lowering doublewides onto basements, pictures of him with company bigwigs. Most of the snapshots, though, pictured us, his family, on elaborate vacations: my sister in Hawaii, me whale-watching, my mother on the main deck of a luxury cruise ship, all of us together on the slopes in Vail. Also present were the bare-chested ladies he met on a topless beach in the Caribbean and the woman swimming in a thong at Club Med. They were all up there as if they were part of our family unit.

His back corner office was filled with awards that lined his walls. He wanted the customers to know that he was a successful, impressive man – a likable, family man who was also the life of the party. Whatever the customer's interest, he did it bigger and better. He always had the upper hand. And according to the books, it contributed to his success. Customers were never dissatisfied. Dad had an inexplicable ability to intimidate and manipulate people while simultaneously surpassing their expectations. He called it customer service, and he took pride in his work.

So it was a big deal when a disgruntled customer came in to voice a complaint. Usually Dad was able to talk to a customer in such a way that the customer got nothing more than he had to begin with but left feeling better about it than when he came in.

*What's that? You thought the interest rate was going to be lower? I had no idea it was going to come back that high. Let me throw in this extra mirror.*

He kept a run-down singlewide "trailer" filled with extra décor for just such occasions.

But it's not every day that an angry customer walked into his office, stood across his desk, pulled out a pistol, and threatened his life. These are the moments that just can't be imagined for a company sales seminar. There is no manual that lesser salesmen can read to know how to handle a man who has just paid tens of thousands of dollars for a home-on-wheels that doesn't have the correct front door or interior paneling or aluminum siding.

He may have been the man-in-charge, but what made Dad successful was, at heart, he was a salesman. Mere salesmen posers would have cowered to the gunman's demands or run away to dial 9-1-1. But not my dad. He knew how to handle people like this. He understood them. He was the only guy in the business who would go through the trouble of setting up a doublewide "trailer" at the county fair. But when it counted, he knew these people. He knew that grown men in Metallica t-shirts and funnel cake-eating women in frayed shorts and fringed leather jackets were likely to pick out their dream home at the county fair. He knew this as a fact just like he knew that posting gaudy, braggadocious snapshots of his family vacations would make him enviable. He knew this just as much as he knew that reacting to this deranged man in fear was the absolute wrong move. Instead, when this disgruntled lunatic decided to barge into my dad's office and negotiate the deal's value compared to my father's life – all from the other end of the six-inch barrel of a pistol pointed at my dad's forehead – my father decided to play a little poker. He called the bluff.

"How about you put that gun down so that we can talk before I come across this desk, take it away from you, and shove it up your ass sideways?" Part of Dad's salesmanship was his amazing way with words. He had a powerful mastery of the common man's vernacular.

I don't know what that man was angry about that day, but I know he left feeling better about the deal than when he came in. And chances are he had nothing more than he did when he came through the door with a revolver shoved down his pants.

On second thought, maybe he walked away with his consolation prize – a gold-framed mirror from the stash in the old singlewide.

# Commando

Options are good. Most people have something that the rest of the world sees as necessary or mandatory that they place in the "optional" category. And different people put different things in that category.

Speed Limits.

The truth.

Manners.

Taxes.

Appropriate, inside voices.

For my dad, it was underwear. I have never known him to wear underwear. Boxers? Briefs? The question was irrelevant to him. He went commando for as long as I can remember. That's not to say that my dad needed underwear any less that the next guy; he just didn't see it that way. As a kid, several times I found myself wishing my dad was not a commando guy.

Awkward moments:

The walk to the neighborhood swimming pool when I looked down and saw what no son ever wants to see poking out the bottom of his father's short shorts. *Come on, Dad, put that away.*

The come-in-here-while-I-try-on-these-pants moments in the dressing room of a department store. *Seriously, Dad, I think I'm better off standing out here by the shoes.*

The early mornings climbing into bed with my parents to start the day off as a happy family. *That one may have traumatized me a bit.*

OK, I gave a full-body shudder as I wrote that.

I imagine that at one time my father flaunted a nice build. I've even seen pictures that prove it. But I remember Dad's physique being like Tony Soprano. Not Tommy Boy, but not exactly Rambo either. He possessed a large diabetic belly so that one could see what contributed to his 280-pound weight only from the side or front. From the back, he looked like a large man…but not fat. He was hairy, and I mean hairy – legs, arms, face, chest, and yes… the back. He was covered. At one time he was plagued by a bald spot on his back that was about the size of a silver dollar, but it eventually filled in too. In an era before the days of metrosexual hairlessness, my father was a real man, proudly displaying his animalism whenever he took off his shirt.

He enjoyed sitting on the couch using his belly as a table for his ice cream, but he couldn't figure out what contributed to his size.

When it came to dressing himself, Dad was particular. He favored wide waist-banded, polyester-blend pants worn at his natural waist near his cavernous belly button.

Age. Bowls of ice cream. Waist size. These things were just numbers to him. He had no problem buying pants possessing a waist size that was double the inseam. Eventually he learned to wear suspenders to keep them up because when you are wearing your pants where your circumference is the greatest, there's just nothing below to stop gravity from doing its thing. But the suspenders didn't become part of his wardrobe until several years after we took a family vacation to the little island of Eleuthera in the Bahamas.

We were at a Club Med resort, and there were all kinds of activities in the sun to occupy our time: swimming pools, tennis, golf…every cliché, resort-life luxury imaginable. But as kids, my sister and I were most interested in learning to water ski. To get to the water skiing area, we had to take a little shuttle bus that dropped us off above a parking lot. We walked down a beautiful pathway to a lower parking lot and out to the dock where we were fitted with life jackets and skis. It was a simple operation run by these creepy tan guys wearing string bikini Speedos whose parents had forgotten to teach them shame. They didn't actually teach anyone much about skiing until that person was in the water holding a rope attached to a boat with a monster truck motor. *Just hang on while these 2,794 horses snatch you out of the water.*

My sister and I braved the clear waters, the tan Speedo-guys, and the powerful motor. After just a couple of days, we were standing on top of two planks riding the wake above the beautiful coral below. Our new nautical adventures took us to the docks most every day we were on vacation there. Despite his size, Dad was a pretty good skier. I had seen him slalom on several occasions. It looked like the Epcot ball riding the monorail. Skiing was nothing new to him. What did pique Dad's interest were the native oranges growing on the trees that lined that beautiful walkway down to the dock. They were big, ripe for the picking. He grabbed one, pulled it off the limb, and tossed it to my mother. *The hairy gorilla thinks of his family first.* He spotted another one and reached for it, coming up short. It dangled there, teasing him with its luscious freshness begging to be peeled – just out of reach. He reached higher. Still it dangled. Still it teased. He stretched as high as he could, but the orange eluded him still. My gorilla-father jumped…

And that's when another family hoping to check out the great skiing in Eleuthera rounded the corner walking down the same path. They seemed a poor, unwary, innocent family with their brood in tow. Perhaps they were also taking in the beauty of the vegetation that lined the path heading down to the waters of the Caribbean, unaware that their senses were about to be assaulted, their innocence ripped from them forever.

My father went up, grabbed the orange, and came down with it firmly in his hand. But when his feet hit the ground, his pants did what things do when there is nothing to stop gravity – they hit the ground shortly after his feet did. There my father stood – completely naked, round, and hairy – declaring to his family, the ambushed family, and everyone else around, that underwear, though optional to him, was still a very good idea.

# The General

We were a skiing family. It started with Dad skiing alone with his friends. Then he started taking me to the local ski resorts when I was about five years old. Later, my little sister joined in the fun; and, finally, my mom, despite her repugnance for the cold, strapped a pair of planks to her feet. On this particular occasion, we were headed to the slopes in Vail, Colorado. Dad had an annual trip to Aspen with his friends, but this was our first family outing out west.

Sure, lots of families take ski vacations to Steamboat, Salt Lake City, Aspen, Copper Mountain, and Vail. But a few dynamics made this vacation a little different from what most families experience. My sister and I, like most middle school kids riding down the road on a family vacation, were hunkered down in the backseat playing games, laughing, singing songs, and occasionally fighting over the imaginary line we had drawn to mark our territories. We just happened to be cruising behind the mystery of blacked-out windows in the back of my father's black Mercedes at 110 miles per hour. Obviously, playing "I Spy" was a little difficult at that speed, but on the bright side, we were making up time after a late start. It may have been a private jet that awaited us at the airport, but it had a schedule to keep, too. And if there is a downside to a private jet, it's the fact that you can't get the airline to book you another flight when you don't make it to the jet-way on time. So there we were, playing our games as if nothing were wrong and blazing down Highway 74 from Shelby to Asheville at Mach 2 in the middle of the night.

We were used to this. Mom was always late it seemed. I don't think I knew until much later in life what the very beginning of a church worship service actually looked like. Wherever we went, we were always in a hurry – not because we had these enormously busy lives but because we were always running late. But when Dad was driving, we made it there on time. We didn't leave any earlier, but let's just say that the trip was always shorter. Dad later explained that, because of the manic extreme of his bipolar disorder, he somehow processed information faster. Everything was fast. He made decisions fast. He drove fast. And when we would finally get to Vail, he would ski fast. Dad rarely found himself in the slower, right-hand lane on a highway. He pretty much stayed in the far left lane…until someone refused to get out of the way. Then he would aggressively jump to the right lane, stomp the accelerator, throw up the finger, and blow past them.

I don't know how he afforded to keep insurance. Later when I would get my driver's license as a teenager, my parents didn't see my insurance as expensive. I guess that was because of all of Dad's tickets. When it came to getting cited by the cops, he was a pro. I have no idea why they never took him to jail over it. So, as we careened down the highway along a darkly-blurred landscape, it wasn't long before Dad looked in his rear view mirror and let some expletives fly. Sure enough, an unmarked cruiser was making a U-turn across the median.

I have no idea what makes some people process information and make decisions so differently from other people. I'm not a neuro-scientist or a psychiatrist. I'm not even really that good at counseling. But I know that some people think they can cross the street in front of buses when the rest of us can see that they are going to die. I know that there have been many people who have accidentally shot their friends. I know there are people who for some reason think they can jump from planes over and over again expecting to consistently cheat death by being strapped to a bed sheet stuffed into a backpack. So while I experienced the results of my dad's decision, I have no idea how he came to make that decision.

After the string of expletives flew from his mouth, the car quickly accelerated. The engine revved as the RPMs climbed higher and higher, and the few cars that were on the road at that hour flashed by much faster. I looked behind us. There were no blue lights. Dad pulled onto an exit ramp. At the stop sign he turned onto a rural road. He drove us a couple miles off the highway and turned down another street. Then he pulled onto the shoulder, slipped the car out of gear, and let the engine idle. *Was this really happening? Had my father really just outrun a North Carolina State Trooper? Were we really sitting here on a desolate street hiding from a cop?*

It didn't feel at all as if I was on a *Dukes of Hazard* episode. My dad's car was hardly the General Lee. It was black, not orange. It was a Benz, not a Dodge. And then, very unlike Bo Duke, my dad opened the car door, got out, and asked my mom to drive.

With mom behind the wheel, Dad instructed her to drive only down back roads, turn after turn into a maze of darkness. Eventually, he advised her to stop the car on some desolate country road. We sat for several minutes just waiting.

After Dad made up his mind that we were safe, he gave Mom permission to return to the highway. He told my sister and me to duck down and hide. *What? Bo would never have asked Daisy to drive so that he could hide from Roscoe!*

Mom reversed our course and turned back onto the highway at a much more reasonable speed. We drove past another exit ramp. No cops. We had lost them. *Really? We had lost them? I was in the eighth grade and I was helping my dad "lose them?"* I started to sit up. "No, stay down until we are sure, kids," he told us. I ducked back down.

Another exit ramp. Then...

Blue lights! They were flashing like crazy and rushing down the ramp after us! Mom slowed down. The cruiser rushed up behind us. Mom pulled over onto the emergency lane and came to a stop. She rolled down her window. The trooper didn't even bother. He walked right up to my dad's window. Dad rolled it down.

"Sir, I need to see your license and registration." Dad gave him the documents.

"Sir, what are you thinking? First, driving 120 miles per hour down this highway. And, did you really think the switch would work? I mean, it may have worked with another car; but we just don't see many of these out here. You don't exactly blend in, you know?"

Dad replied, "We're just trying not to miss our flight out of Asheville."

Dad got out of the car, along with my mom. They changed places again. My sister and I sat back up in the back seat.

The trooper gave my dad his license along with a warning ticket. "Just do me a favor and try to keep it under 100."

He learned his lesson that night. Fast driving is fine; quick, outrageous explanations are even better.

# Name Change

Opposites attract. It's a cliché, I know. But it's true of my parents. My father drove a very high-profile, take-notice-of-me luxury car. My mother drove a Toyota Tercel. My father bought me expensive leather jackets. My mother took me shopping in the budget department. My father threw handfuls of silver tinsel *at* the Christmas tree. My mother deliberately and gently placed one piece of tinsel on one carefully-chosen branch at a time. My father enjoyed steak. My mother loved hot dogs. My father bought a full-length mink coat for my mother. She kept it hidden in the back of her closet. I learned most of the curse words in the English language from listening to my father speak. When I came home from school and asked my mother what the F-word meant, she read a book to me about copulating hamsters. Opposites attract.

My mother once made me return a Poison poster because the guys in the band were dressed in drag. My father owned an X-rated drive-in movie theater and porn shop. My mom wouldn't let us go in the shop. My dad often let us go in and help him count money.

I lived in these two worlds that were blended by my juxtaposed parents. Climbing out of the big black Benz to help my dad count money in the porn shop on Saturday. Climbing out of the little red Tercel to study the Bible at church on Sunday.

They were both involved in my childhood...in their own way. Mom was always the Class Mother at school. She brought snacks to all the children, organized all the parties, volunteered in the classroom, and went on every field trip I can remember. Dad's business sponsored my Little League baseball team. I assumed other dads did the same thing. Their teams were named after local businesses like Parkdale or BB&T. My team was always named after my dad's eyebrow-raising business: Sky Vue Theater.

It was really exciting. In T-ball, we were the Sky Vue Mets. In Little League we were the Sky Vue Cardinals. I remember being in the front yard while Dad opened these big white boxes to reveal the bright green and gold uniforms for the Mets and the bright red and pure white uniforms for the Cardinals. We had real uniforms, complete with real baseball jerseys, real baseball pants, real baseball socks, real baseball caps. We looked great… like pro players. But instead of our names being printed on the backs of our jerseys, they read "Sky Vue Theater." The kid on the mound, what's his name? Sky Vue. The kid out in center field, what's his name? Sky Vue. The kid behind the plate? Sky Vue. The snotty-nosed kid sitting the bench? Sky Vue. I was so proud.

As sponsor, Dad had several responsibilities. He bought all the uniforms. He bought all the equipment – catcher's pads, bats, balls, whatever. He paid any fees. He provided the post-game snacks. He provided the post-season party. And he provided the ever-sought-after, post-season trophies. We had great gear! We had fantastic pool parties! We had tasty snacks! And we had big trophies! Go big, or go home!…compliments of my dad and Sky Vue.

When I reflect back on those days, I can't figure out why other parents were okay with Dad's sponsorship of our team. I've seen parents boycott Disney. I've seen parents stand together demanding censorship in music. I've seen books removed from school libraries. I've seen parents effectively demand that Abercrombie stop marketing thongs to elementary girls. Maybe no one knew what to do. Maybe they were petrified from the shock. Maybe, like me, they just liked the bright colors and the pool party…the seemingly bottomless pocketbook.

Both my parents were there...in their own way. Mom was always there at the games cheering me on. Whether I was playing first base or second-string right field, she was there…cheering in the stands. Dad was there too, but you couldn't see him…unless you looked on the backs of 12 kids wearing really sharp uniforms. We had all changed our names.

# Backyard Buckshot

Sons want to please their fathers. Sons want to be their dads' best friends. Sons desire treats and praise from their fathers. Me? I frequently retrieved things for my dad.

*Son, get me that ice cream from the freezer.*

*Hey, where's the Channel Master?* (That's what he called the TV remote.)

(Yelling from the shower) *Jonathan, bring me a dry towel.*

So, it was natural that when Dad went hunting that I knew my role. He adorned me in a coat with big pockets and dispatched me to run across the fields and retrieve the birds he shot out of the air. I was the faithful Labrador, hoping for a word of praise or the gift of an ice cream sandwich as I ran back across the field to him after retrieving his dead birds with their limp bodies flopping in my pockets.

But there came a time when Dad quit leaving the house to shoot things. Our yard had become a Mecca for squirrels making their holy pilgrimage to gather the thousands of acorns that fell from the huge oaks. They were a nuisance – both the acorns and the squirrels. The squirrels had even begun finding ways into our attic where they chewed on wires and left droppings all over the floor. One of them had died between the walls and left behind the smell of decaying rodent. Whether we trapped them, poisoned them, or executed them, they had to go.

We didn't live in the city limits. We didn't have curbside trash service, and we had to depend on the volunteer fire department. But county living had its perks too. We had fewer taxes, and we could shoot whatever we wanted in our yard. Dad had started taking pride in his lack of subtlety, and I found myself standing at his side on the back deck while he raised a 20-gauge to his shoulder and began picking off the bushy-tailed rodents in the backyard. When he shot them, they flipped up in the air like an Olympic gymnast.

Our neighbors were from upstate New York and were not accustomed to having neighbors killing things next door. They rather marveled in the novelty of those pesky squirrels. Dad enjoyed seeing the horror on the city-slickers' faces each time he dropped one of those tree rats. And just when the neighbors were starting to get used to it, Dad upped the ante. It must have been an ominous sight: the prep schoolboy dressed in camouflage and gripping a gleaming hatchet, standing beside his father who was armed with a shotgun.

Many of my friends had deer heads mounted above their fireplaces. I remember walking across their living rooms noticing how those black eyes followed me, watching me beneath their impressive racks. Dead, yet alive. My bedroom wall was similar. But instead of deer heads mounted by professional taxidermists, my wall had stiffened, decaying squirrel tails that I had chopped off with my little hatchet and hung with Scotch tape.

Make no mistake: Dad's dispatch of his son to chop off squirrel tails in front of his New Yorker neighbors was all about putting on a show. He liked to have the upper hand, and one thing Dad employed often in his arsenal of intimidation was shock.

And if he had to knock down a few tree rats to make sure the neighbors knew their place, well…I was ready with my hatchet.

# The Abyss

When I was a child, I hit my best friend in the face with a baseball bat, and I still have a hard time believing it actually happened. And blowing up a frog with a bottle rocket? I can't believe I did that either. But the most notable did-that-really-just-happen moment of my childhood occurred on the backside of a 10-day family vacation in Hawaii.

The first part was filled with the excitement of the very touristy Oahu, featuring fire shows and hula dances at the Polynesian Culture Center; zipping through the streets of Honolulu on motorized scooters; an insane music-themed helicopter ride with a pilot who assaulted mountains, cliffs, and beaches as if he was Maverick in *Top Gun*; the weird old guy in the gross thong on Waikiki Beach; the creepy feeling of looking down at the sunken *USS Arizona* knowing all those dead sailors were entombed below; and the insanity of clinging to the trampoline of a racing Catamaran as she suddenly heeled up at a 45 degree angle and launched like a rocket in the winds swirling around Diamond Head.

The adventure was over and we were heading to the lush and boring island of Maui to wrap up the vacation with a hearty yawn. I was anticipating the excitement of watching for falling coconuts. Mom was excited about watching some whales, but cruising on a big boat doing an impressive two knots while looking at a few masses of blubber through binoculars sounded about as exciting as a lecture on photosynthesis from Charlie Brown's teacher.

When we strolled up to the dock, we found that our big boat was, in reality, a rubber raft with a rusty motor strapped to it. It was complemented by a guy at the "helm" who looked a lot like the crazy fisherman from *Jaws* and insisted on being called "Captain." It wasn't long, and we were slamming through the waves and swells with nothing but our butts to grip the side of the raft. About the time there was nothing in sight – no more boats, no more land – Captain Crazy Eyes shut off the engine and announced we had arrived. Just like we'd pulled up in Grandma's driveway. *Great job, Captain, on finding the driveway; it's only 4,376 miles wide!* There was nothing but water. Water everywhere. If the raft sprang a leak, we were all going to die. I spoke up, "How deep is it here?" I don't know why, but I always ask that. It's like asking a dentist all the things that could go wrong if the drill slips. It's not a good question. Nothing good comes from that question. It's best not to think about these things when you've surrendered to the expertise of a man who looks as if he may have just been released from prison.

We all looked around. One would think that a whale-watching excursion would involve some whales. Nope. Nothing. There was water. Lots of water. As far down as you'd like to imagine, there was water. But there were no whales. The boat – I mean raft – rocked and squeaked as it drifted over the swells. And we just sat there gripping the side of that raft and looking for a sign of life. When water is that deep, it changes colors. The deeper it gets – even the clear blue water of Maui – it almost turns black. A morbid, evil, gothic black. Shadows move under the surface and there's no way of knowing if it's a fish, a sea monster, or the shelf of an unholy abyss. My imagination did strange things despite my attempts to shut it down. Captain Crazy Eyes apparently expected to see something while we were out there. He was getting nervous, apologizing that there were no whales. "This hasn't ever happened," he kept saying. "There's always something out here."

*Yeah, I'm sure there is, Captain. Can we go now?*

Just as we were accepting the fact that this whole excursion had been a waste of money and a big disappointment, I noticed a shimmering blue arc among the shadows beneath us. I have no way of telling you how disconcerting that is. But it's one of those moments where you don't want to be alone. So I asked, "Captain, what's that down there?"

And that question brought Captain Crazy Eyes back to life. "Oh my God, that's one of them! That's a humpback whale!"

In water that deep, when you see something below you, you have no real idea how far down it is. It looked close, but how could you really know? Driven by hope, I assumed it was approximately 243 feet down. The alternative was inconceivable. As if on cue, the whale rose beneath us. It came up and breached not six feet from us. It was huge. I mean HUGE. Seeing one in a museum can't do justice to seeing one in the wild like that, six feet from your rubber raft with no sight of land. The gigantic beast did its blowhole thing right there beside us. You could feel the mist from its spray. The Captain was no longer the scariest part of this picture.

The day I hit my best friend in the face with a baseball bat? I can explain that. The day Eric and I killed that frog? I can try to explain that. But what happened next on that rubber raft I will never comprehend.

It happened so fast. My father stood up, picked up his fourteen-year-old son, and threw me into the water with that whale.

Most dads would be thrilled to take in the serene magnitude with their sons, marveling at the beauty and power of such a creature – maybe catch it on video or on camera. Most dads would take a careful but quick inventory to make sure everyone was safely away from the edge of the boat. But, not mine. Mine chucked me into the abyss with that monster.

I've heard stories about the power of adrenaline kicking in and helping mom's lift cars off their kids. And I'm telling you, I believe it. Because in that moment, the impossible happened. It must have been the power of that adrenaline because I suddenly became like a fourteen-year-old merman – without the trident or long white beard – and I did one of those big full-body fish kicks and propelled myself back over the side of that boat like a spawning salmon.

I was terrified.

Mom was horrified.

Dad just laughed.

I guess he thought watching whales was boring too.

# The Hussy Derby

To assert boldness, one must remove subtlety from his personality. My Dad executed subtlety long ago.

In Dad's young adult days, he enjoyed hanging out in the bar at his favorite fishing peer at the beach. His confidence and hairiness contributed to his swagger, and he found himself at the end of many a lady's gaze in that bar. One night, when Dad was feeling abnormally introspective, he was sitting at the bar, keeping his eyes to himself when a lady walked in and sat down a few stools down. Sipping his beer, Dad resisted the urge to give her the look. Another man decided to fill the vacuum and walked up to her, asking, "Hey there, sweetie, you wanna dance?"

"No, thanks," she answered.

The other guy was persistent and placed his hand on her back. "Oh, one dance can't hurt."

"I really don't want to," she answered.

"What's wrong, honey? I'll show you a good time."

And that's when Dad decided to break stride.

"Hey, I believe the lady's spoken for."

The guy turned toward Dad and asked, "Why don't you mind your own business. This is none of your concern."

"You need to leave her alone. She's already said she doesn't want to dance with you."

"Yeah? And what are you gonna do about it?"

Dad answered him with a beer mug to his face and dragged his unconscious body outside onto the beach. Words are subtler than action, and Dad was no fan of subtlety.

Take, for example, an average Saturday trip to the skating rink. Kate's Skating Rink was a big deal. Kate's had a disco ball and a black light. They had a birthday clown. Everyday the staff instructed all the kids to sit in a circle and play a toned-down version of Spin the Bottle with a bowling pin. The winner received a free box of stale popcorn or rectangular slice of school pizza. Kate's did the Hokey Pokey and left no doubt they knew what it was all about. There was no skating rink in the country more legit – ahem…cliché – than Kate's.

Mom had a pair of white figure skates, and she was gracefully amazing. My sister and I were stuck with the hideous beaver-brown rentals with 70s orange wheels. I couldn't dance worth anything, but with some Michael Jackson blaring and some disco lights flashing when I was skating that endless wooden oval, I could find a snappy little bobbing groove. Dad, though, had a sweet pair of black leather speed skates with custom wheels and bearings – size 12. Sure, he was pretty fast, but more importantly, Dad could do something on skates that most guys couldn't…something that moved a guy way up the mojo ladder…the one thing that was sure to make the ladies swoon. Dad could skate backwards.

For a young elementary school boy, the point of skating was speed. Run on your toe-stops at the whistle. Break into a powerful, arm-swinging stride. Execute the perfect crossover during the turns. And stay low. Always stay low. There was nothing else. Because speed outdistanced style, most guys didn't learn to skate backwards. But while they endured ridicule when young, it definitely paid off for the very few who did learn. Because when it came to the menacing "couple's skate," no one had more game than the backward skaters. When a guy can skate backwards, he doesn't have to settle for holding just one hand. He's rewarded with the much more intimate and impressive "double-hand embrace."

On this particular Saturday at Kate's Skating Rink, I was standing there positioned just off the rink during the couple's skate scratching my head and wondering about this strange woman with whom my father was skating backwards. She wasn't wearing a pair of white figure skates. Her hair was different. It sure wasn't my mother. It was not the woman that loved our family and whistled for me to come home at suppertime – the woman who greeted me after school with a Little Debbie cake. This was someone else. She was with my dad. She was shamelessly engaging him with the "double-hand embrace." Who was this mystery woman at the center of the attention my father garnered with his backward roller-skating prowess?

When Dad took me home that day, I asked my mom who that lady was. And that was the day I found out what adultery was.

Subtle, my father was not.

# Kitty, Kitty

This is a really embarrassing confession, but I'll admit it. We were a cat family. My friends had dogs – German Shepherds, Saint Bernards, Black Labs. We had cats. Lots of them. Sure, we had some dogs along the way, but none of them lasted long. Here's a brief history of our dogs:

Dewey – a cairn terrier that we got rid of because he farted too much.

Stinger – a pit bull that we got rid of because of his sociopathic tendencies.

Jumper – a wired-hair terrier that got shot.

That's it. That's the entire list of dogs we owned from my entire childhood. None of them lasted for more than a few months. Now cats, on the other hand. That's an entirely different story. The list is much more robust:

Beep Beep – named by yours truly when I was a toddler, presumably because it was one of the only things I could say.

Funny Face – named after, well…her face.

Susan – named after one of my teachers.

Snowball – she was white.

Dudley – also white, named by my father after Dudley brand softballs.

Pearl – guess what color she was.

Fuzz – a long-haired white cat who was scared of heights.

Lolly – named as such because my parents thought saying her name really loud when calling her was fun.

Precious – appropriately named because of her amputated ears.

We were a cat family. And our cats were weird. Funny face was the ugliest cat I have ever seen. Her front legs were shorter than her back legs, but that was hardly noticeable because of her face. Susan was the dumbest cat I have ever encountered. She had kittens while she was still nursed by her own mother, the ugly Funny Face. Susan didn't even know to lick the amniotic sac off her kittens after they were born. Apologies to my teacher. We had no idea she was so stupid when we named her. Dudley was completely deaf. Pearl was attacked by the neighbor's dog and shaken until her guts had to be sewn back together in a little emergency procedure. She was always a little jumpy after that incident. Fuzz frightened easily. He regularly pooped his fur when other cats walked up. It was a little on the disgusting side. Lolly and Precious had been rescued from a house fire. Lolly was fairly normal. Precious had lost the pads on her paws because of the fire. And her ears, also burned, developed gangrene and had to be amputated. The base of her ears still turned quickly as she tried to determine where noise was coming from.

Dad's contribution to the list of cats was Snowball. She was a rescue cat he had adopted from work – the X-rated, drive-in, movie theater. Dad referred to her as "Whore Cat." Looking back on the circumstances – where she came from and the fact that she was the first in a long line of white cats – I think it was an appropriate term. If not appropriate, at least it was accurate. If you could think of a cat who had been rescued from an X-rated theater and porn shop, I guess Snowball fit the bill. Like I said, she was constantly pregnant. And while she paled in comparison to Susan's stupidity, she wasn't the sharpest claw on the paw either. Like all cats, trees attracted Snowball. She liked to climb them. When dogs chased her, up the tree she went. When cars drove by, she ran right up again. Part cat, part skank, part squirrel. That was Snow Ball. But as annoying as she was, Dad had a really soft spot in his heart for her.

Dad spent a lot of time at work, and it was fairly common for my mom to take my sister and me down to spend a few days with my grandparents. It was a five-hour trip, so we always tried to stay for a few days. Dad stayed at home, did the work thing, and fed the cats. At the time, that was Funny Face, Susan, and Snowball. Ugly. Stupid. And Slut.

Well, it didn't take long for Snowball to get a little nervous. While Dad was off at work, something happened that sent Snowball up the tree again. But this time it must have been something terribly frightening because she clamored way up the tree. When Dad came home and got out of the car, he began hearing Snowball's cry. He walked around looking for her, and that's when he noticed that the cry was coming from above. Snowball was in the tree – a massive oak tree. Normally she just went up the trunk and hung there until whatever threat had passed. But this time she was way up in the branches hanging on for dear life. He called her. She cried. He called her. She tried to come down. But alas, she was stuck. She could get up there. But she couldn't get down because she was petrified with fear. He continued to call. She continued to hang on. It was a stale mate. The stupid slut-cat and her rescuing pimp.

Dad did not like heights. He didn't do ladders, roofs, or hotel balconies. I remember one day when Dad had a crew of men with a bucket truck to repair the screen at the movie theater. He was fine sending me thirty feet up in that bucket, but no one could cajole him to take a ride in it. He and heights were not friends. Dad was also the kind of man who had no trouble calling for help. If the sink leaked, he called a plumber. If the car was leaking oil, he took it to a mechanic. If the grass needed to be cut, he called a landscaper. If the light bulbs needed changing, he called someone else. On this particular day when he realized he could not coax Snowball out of that big oak, he did the most logical thing he could think of. He called the Fire Department. And they showed up. Ladders. Hoses. Trucks. Oxygen Tanks. The whole nine yards. Parked right there in our driveway. They brainstormed ideas until they had developed a plan they could actually implement, and eventually Snowball found herself in the grasp of a fireman at the top of a ladder. Of course, she was scared. And when cats get scared, they flail and scratch and squirm. Unable to safely carry her down the ladder without her jumping or falling, the firemen went to phase 2 of the plan. Out came the big trampoline. A group of them congregated beneath her holding the trampoline while the fireman on the ladder took aim. Then, with my dad watching, the fireman held Snowball out and let go.

Dad described her as a flying squirrel, spreading all four legs as she descended – like a skydiver attempting to slow his plummet to earth. Snowball landed on the trampoline feet first. She took one big bounce, landed again, and ran off.

Sure, Dad ran a sketchy, X-rated, drive-in movie theater. And, yes, the external door of his office may have been adorned with the faces of porn stars. But deep down, Dad held to some good 'ole 1950s community values. He knew how to call the fire department for a slutty, treed cat.

# The Steed

Some people collect stamps. Or little silver spoons. Or those creepy Russian nutcrackers. Or maybe cats. My dad collected some things too:

Guns.

Coins.

Polyester-blend polos.

And speeding tickets.

Over a surprisingly short amount of time, he amassed fourteen of those…unpaid. Eventually the value of those tickets rendered a bonus arrest warrant. For a good while he ignored the tickets, along with the warrant, and kept driving. Perhaps he was hoping to expand the collection and cash in on the Antique Road Show. But when the cops impounded his car, he had to say goodbye to that freedom. For a few years he dreamed of getting it back. He would occasionally window shop for cars. He had a hard time accepting reality…or laws.

But then came the rediscovery of freedom: a Power Wheelchair. It was kind of like the "Next-time-I'm-going-to-the-Grand-Canyon" Hoveround, but it was much bigger. Dad liked his speed. So he got a chair that ran off two oversized batteries and topped out near 20 mph. It was a beast in the elevators.

He acquired his suped-up, four-wheeled steed with a little under-the-table racket arranged with the wheelchair company. Most people possess this thing called shame. My dad did not. He knew nothing of embarrassment. So in this business arrangement, Dad used his incredibly intense talent he had for sales. He did this by standing outside doctors' offices and hospitals soliciting interest from people who had Medicaid or Medicare. With a talent for striking up a conversation with drug dealers and disabled veterans alike, he would show them his tricked-out ride and explain to them how they could get one of their own for free. He'd get their contact information and pass it to his man on the inside in exchange for cash. He got $200 for each chair he "sold." And Dad could sell. Call it an exercise in creativity. He was really big with the maimed-diabetic-smoker crowd.

The chair – that's what he called it – gave him some freedom. But his shamelessness took him to extremes. And the extremes contributed to several of his predominant problems:

Social problems, like when he took corners too close at the speed of sound, running his hot rod of a wheelchair through walls.

Liability problems, like when he disappeared from a post-op rehab facility and became the subject of a citywide APB while he went on a Wal-Mart shopping spree seven miles away.

Safety problems, like when the cops pulled him over driving his wheelchair in the emergency lane along the eight-lane I-85 corridor, but not before he made it out of Charlotte and across the county line.

When he still had his license, safety wasn't a concern of Dad's. He never wore a seatbelt. I never saw him use a turn signal. And he obviously never obeyed speed limits. That translated to his operation of The Chair. He didn't use one of those orange, triangle-shaped safety flags. And when he ran out of sidewalk, he just seized the road as if he owned it. A king riding his great padded throne on wheels at 20 miles per hour…at night…with no lights.

When it comes to worrying about him, I'm at a loss. For some reason, his scurrying around in that wheelchair all seemed natural at the time. Maybe it was the way he explained himself. Maybe we simply looked the other way. Maybe we were all used to his lack of logic. Maybe we knew there was no way he'd listen to anyone anyway. Maybe I chose not to care because he had more lives than a demon cat straight from the pits of Hell. By this time the man had walked away from a 170 mph car crash across three lanes of interstate. He had survived multiple drug overdoses and an attempt to gas himself in the garage. He lived on the constant edge of a diabetic coma. He had beaten colon cancer. He had walked away from a missed drunken back flip on a ski jump. Even when he willed it, it appeared the man could not die. In the back of our minds we had all started to wonder just how many lives this man could have.

I remember joking with my wife: "You know, he'll probably end up getting hit by a car on that stupid wheelchair. And that's how he'll die." We said it for years while he "drove" to his doctor appointments and scooted down to the store for chocolate milk.

On one trip to the store, crossing the road, it happened. He didn't look, and sure enough, this helpless old guy's sedan found out what happens when you tangle with a shameless, chocolate milk-guzzling, chain-smoking maniac in a suped-up power wheelchair. The car was smashed. The chair was totaled. Dad had cut his foot.

Chalk up another life for the maniacal demon cat.

He did the logical thing; he ordered a bigger chair.

# Catch Me If You Can

When my wife and I got married, we had two cars. One was a white Honda CRX that I learned was giving me carbon monoxide poisoning from its shoddy exhaust system. The other was a white, three-cylinder Geo Prism 4-door that we called "The Pebble" (Chevrolet owned Geo, and since the car wasn't quite *Like a Rock*, we opted for a step down in nomenclature). At any rate, after my wife blew up all three cylinders by running the oil bone dry (She had been checking the transmission fluid instead of the oil, but that shouldn't matter because I have since learned "that's not her job anyway"), we decided to purchase a new-to-us car. We settled on a 1995 Saturn that was – you guessed it – white. We sat down with the bank to finance the car and found out there was a problem. Apparently, I had an unpaid credit card from a department store called Dillard's. The problem lied in the fact that I had never applied for, received, or used a credit card through Dillard's. It took only a moment for me to figure out what the problem was. A little problem spelled D-A-D.

I should have seen it coming. Dad had just gone through a period where his interest in my social security number was a little more than cavalier. I had even started to become uncomfortable with the frequency of his phone calls asking about it:

Phone rings.

"Hello?" I answer.

"What's your social security number?" he asks. No niceties. No segue. He just jumped straight to it.

The next week:

Phone rings.

"Hey, Dad."

"Hey, Son."

"How's it going?" I ask.

"Were you born in 1976?"

"No, Dad. 1974."

"And what are the last four digits of your social security number?"

Over and over, that's the way it went. Sure, I thought something might be up, but I blew it off. And when for Christmas he had spent four hundred dollars each on my mom, my sister, and me – money I knew he didn't have since he was homeless – I thought absolutely nothing about it. I didn't have much money because I was fresh out of college; and, really – what father steals his son's identity in order to buy that same son a bunch of Christmas gifts? Well, apparently mine did. And, along with the sack of gifts from "Dear Ole' Santa," I was also holding the proverbial bag of financial consequences brought on by Dad's "generosity."

Dad never let anything stop him from getting what he wanted. In this case, he wanted to be able to be a big spender for his family at Christmas. Most people, I guess, wouldn't know how to steal someone else's identity, much less have the nerve to actually do it. But Dad? He didn't just steal some random guy's identity; he stole his son's identity and stuck that son with the bill. You have to give him credit: once he made a decision, he was all in. No fear of commitment. Follow-through? That's a different story. But when it came to jumping in with both feet, Dad did not hesitate. He always got his, whatever it took.

A few years after I resolved the blemish from Dad's little stroll down Steal-Your-Son's-Identity Road, he was again in a tight spot. The circumstances were a little more dismal. This time it wasn't an inability to buy Christmas gifts but an inability to pay for his medication. He was no longer homeless, but he had some problems with his Medicare Part D healthcare plan that was commonly referred to as "the donut hole." With Dad's build and frame, coupled with his regular sugar intake, I assumed he would look upon anything called a "donut hole" pretty favorably. But it had nothing to do with sweets. The "donut hole" commonly referred to the point at which one's Medicare benefits reached their limit and quit paying for medical attention. Dad needed more medical attention than Dolly Parton needs wigs. So when dad hit the "donut hole" and found himself responsible for 100% of his prescription costs, it was a real problem. Dad was desperate. He had no money for his prescriptions, and he had blown through the samples he received from the doctors.

When Dad failed to take his medication or couldn't take his medication, the voices in his head became more disturbing – both in the number of them and the things they said. Those voices told him things about himself that he listened to. They were the kinds of voices that tell a person he is sober when he clearly isn't; the kinds of voices that tell a man his porn-stache is sexy; the kinds of voices that tell a man there's nothing wrong with wearing suspenders without a shirt. Crazy voices. And while Dad could feel great when he was manic, the depression drop always landed him in the psych ward following yet another fruitless suicide attempt – one more thing he felt he couldn't get right. While "donut" normally brings to mind things like Hot Signs, sprinkles, Bavarian cream, jelly filling, coffee, and cops; for my dad, the donut was a really low point of each year – the kind of low point that would make even a completely sane man consider some very insane actions. Considering sanity wasn't one of those things in Dad's strong suit, it also became a perilously unsure time of the year for him – an expectantly unpredictable time of the year for those around him.

The setting: Home Depot. Dad was well into the donut hole. His stockpile of samples had been depleted. Things were getting ugly.

Enter: Dad's unique application of logic. He thought about the places where he knew he could get his meds. There were two he could think of. First was the hospital. He could overdose again and land a comfy stay in a locked-down ward. But to overdose, he needed pills. Dead end there. The other place to get free medication was jail. And to go to jail, he simply had to do something illegal. Jackpot! That was something in which Dad excelled. That is what took Dad and his power wheelchair into Home Depot that day. He marched (err, rolled) right down the main aisle, his mind determined to leave that parking lot handcuffed like Lindsay Lohan in the backseat of a squad car. With his mind's eye on the prized jail cell, with the pesky voices in his head, and with a new resolve for criminal activity, Dad pondered what he needed to steal to warrant a 9-1-1 call. A fat man in a wheelchair isn't likely to pull off a smash and grab at the customer service desk. But, a nice set of screwdrivers could work. No, not enough value to get enough jail time. A high-end drill? What about a fichus tree? Or a paint sprayer? A mailbox? What about a nail gun?

He made his decision.

The wheelchair accented his physical issues as he bolted for the door as fast as his little four solid wheels could carry him. But it was the massive microwave oven in his lap that pointed to his emotional state.

*Come on, Dad. Really? A microwave? A store full of smaller, easier-to-carry big-ticket items, and you chose a microwave?*

He got his meds.

Voices silenced. Mood swings stabilized. Blood sugar normalized.

He was fully committed. Mission accomplished.

# Supplemental Interlude: His Ailments

*because an appendix belongs only at the end*

# Supplemental Interlude: His Ailments

Many of Dad's antics – especially the gross ones that follow – were in some way related to the numerous ailments and disorders that plagued him. When people would ask me what kinds of medical conditions he faced, I frequently answered, "Most of them." And then to prove a point, I'd challenge them to name something that could be wrong with someone, and when they named the first things that came to mind, I could always count on being able to say, "Yeah, he has that." But in reality, it's not true to say that he was plagued with almost everything. There are several conditions he didn't have. For one, he was never pregnant.

So here's a list:

*Obesity.* He was a big man. This was mostly because he liked to eat. And he ate a lot. Some of his favorite foods were Zero candy bars, snow cones, steak, pork rinds, and fried okra. We took him to eat at a Shoney's one time just a couple years before he died, and my vegetarian daughter watched in horror as Dad consumed four pieces of sausage, four pieces of toast, and eight runny eggs that he sopped up with my daughter's leftover French fries.

*Diabetes.* When he was first diagnosed with diabetes, he tried to control it with pills. He refused to change his diet and moved on to insulin shots. I don't know if he reused his needles. But I know he reused his glucose lancets. He just used them until they were too dull to bring up any blood. The diabetes led to some other big problems, like…

*Neuropathy.* He had no feeling in his feet. At first it just made him a little wobbly when he walked. Then it complicated when he would run over his foot with his wheelchair and tear open a wound, leading to…

*Diabetic ulcers.* It seems like they got worse as he got older. And I can hardly remember a time when he wasn't battling one or two during his later years. All I know is they smelled horrible and, in some cases, gaped clear down to the bone. He visited the hospital a good bit because of the ulcers, and the doctors regularly discharged him with massive amounts of antibiotics for the open wound they were strategically allowing to drain. I felt sorry for the home health nurses that changed the bandages. The infection eventually led to…

*Amputation.* Nothing major, just a few toes and part of a foot. By the time it happened he had already resolved to depend upon the wheelchair for mobility. So it didn't hinder him from walking. Flip-flops could have been a problem, but Dad hated them most of his life and had long since stopped wearing shoes of any kind anyway.

*Renal failure.* His kidneys were shutting down. This is another condition that stemmed from the diabetes. He refused dialysis. And there were several times that we thought he was going to die only to find that his kidneys had cranked back up again. They proved to be some astoundingly resilient organs.

*Toe fungus.* Even when he was young he had gross toenails. They were yellow, thick, jagged, and crumbly. There was not a single fungus-free toe on either foot. It only got worse with the foot problems he had going on.

*Cancer.* It was in his colon. He didn't like to talk about it. But I think anyone who was around ended up having to deal with some of the symptoms. He went through a dirty diaper-throwing phase at one of the facilities that cared for him. There was one nurse in particular that he didn't like. He liked to target her with the diapers. Bless her.

*Methicillin-resistant Staphylococcus aureus.* This is called MRSA for short. It's pronounced mursa. It's a kind of staff infection that is very difficult to treat because it almost dares antibiotics to take a stab at it. It was disturbing when the doctors first informed us of this condition when they instructed us to wear biohazard suits when visiting him in the hospital. It's hard to reassure someone that everything's going to be okay when you are dressed like they have a zombie virus.

*Drug addiction.* It started with alcohol. But then his dentist friend introduced him to cocaine back in the 80s as "the rich man's drug." Dad got hooked. It destroyed his nasal passages. So he switched to crack. It destroyed the rest of him.

*Schizophrenia.* Sometimes he said he could actually hear the drugs calling out his name. Sometimes he just saw little green men running up and down his walls. For a long time, the doctors thought these episodes were symptomatic of his drug abuse; but eventually the doctors determined that he suffered from schizophrenia. The drug use, however, was always a contributing factor and exacerbated the problem.

*Bipolar disorder.* Most of the time he was on a manic swing. The manic swings were characterized by spending lots of money, driving fast cars at insane speeds, punching the VP of the company in the face, and dancing with strange women. When dad was manic, it was simply impossible to out-think him. Doctors explained that Dad was so manic that the coke actually calmed him down. I still don't understand that. The other side of the coin – depression – often led him to a suicide attempt…usually with a surplus of pills. Dad didn't like blood.

*Cardiomegaly.* That's an enlarged heart. Don't let it fool you: an enlarged heart does not mean it's stronger. An enlarged heart leads to increased abdominal girth (yep), weight gain (yep), fatigue (yep), and shortness of breath (panting?). And what leads to an enlarged heart? Lots of things can cause it, but Dad's big-ticket item was cocaine abuse.

*Insomnia.* We're not sure what caused it. It could have been the cocaine. Or the plethora of other medications' effects on him. Our maybe it was the gunshots in the neighborhoods he eventually called home. Whatever the reason, Dad had a really hard time sleeping. He started taking Ambien. And Dad liked to self-medicate. So he got multiple prescriptions for the same drug. He started taking more and more of it. It was dangerous, but it was also a little entertaining to call him after he had knocked himself out for the night at 6:00. He'd answer the phone completely out of his mind, talking about the aliens in his room or the helicopter he just flew down to Greenville, South Carolina. Good times.

*Tooth Decay.* When I was a kid, Dad had several gold crowns. Later, when I was in middle school, he got his coked-up dentist friend to redo all of his teeth with these really expensive white caps. He had a great smile. But over so many years of drug use, especially when he switched to crack, the tooth decay cranked back up. He spent the last few years of his life without any teeth. Some dentist had convinced him to have them ALL extracted. I never understood why. Dad said it had something to do with Medicare and insurance. I'm not sure he understood it either.

*Glaucoma.* He got to where he couldn't see much of anything. He had some drops to help with it, but he couldn't really see to apply them. Most of the time it was OK. But we all worried a little at the thought of him driving that powered wheelchair to the store, especially when he could just see big blurs and shapes without any detail. It was easy for him to mistake holes for oil spots…or speeding dump trucks for large, stampeding land mammals.

# The Second Trashbag:
# His Gross Antics

> *Tragedy is when I cut my finger;*
> *comedy is when you fall into an open sewer and die.*
> — *Mel Brooks*

# Put A Sock On It

I must admit that I have always been a little judgmental of those women who go to Wal-Mart in their bedroom shoes. It's not that you have to get all gussied up to go buy soap or toilet paper or whatever, but everyone has a line. My line is shoes. Flip-flops? Fine. Work boots? Fine. I don't really care what kind of shoes. I'm even okay with the kids who wear their cleats after a t-ball game. But bedroom slippers? Come on.

My wife put meaning to this for me years ago when she pointed out that you could tell a lot about a person by the shoes she is wearing. And maybe it's a weird thing, but one of the first things I have always noticed on a person is shoes. I even remember how excited my Kindergarten teacher's assistant was when I complimented her shoes. Some people notice what color eyes someone has after meeting her for the first time. Others remark on hairstyles. Some can remember the first, middle, and last name. Some take note of the shirt. Me? I notice the shoes. My wife is right about reading people that way, and through the years I've gained confidence that I had it right all along. It's true: You can tell a lot about a person based on the shoes.

As a kid, we liked to vacation at Wrightsville Beach. Wrightsville is not commercialized like Myrtle or Daytona. It's largely residential. We would park the car on one of the side streets that had beach access and walk to the sand. The sand was hot, but it was a relief from the heat of the blacktop. Leaving our shoes in the car, I remember balancing on the white or yellow lines to save our feet the agony of the heat trapped by the black tar in the asphalt. During those years of beach combing, I learned a valuable lesson:

walking barefoot on asphalt isn't quite like walking on hot coals, but it's pretty close.

Interestingly, one of the most definitive moments in how I saw my dad came when I realized he had made the decision not to wear shoes…ever.

He had decided not to wear shoes because he could hardly walk due to his struggle with diabetes…

Okay, I better stop right there. *Struggle* probably isn't the best word. *Neglect* is probably a better word. He knew he had diabetes for years. He "controlled" it with food and insulin. That means that if his sugar was low, he ate lots of sugar. And if it was high, which it usually was, he took massive amounts of insulin to bring it down. If his meter said his glucose levels were at 400, that was not a big deal. He could take enough insulin to drop that back down. Dad always had his own way of doing things.

After years of self-treating his diabetes with this roller coaster ride of insulin and sugar, Dad had lost all the feeling in his feet. Balance becomes more difficult when you can't feel your feet. Walking becomes more challenging when you can't balance. It would seem completely logical to most people that buying a scooter when you don't have feeling in your feet is a bad idea; but to Dad, riding a scooter merely requires you to be able to sit and push the throttle.

My parents had a rule for us when we were growing up. Before the days of bicycle helmets and kids roller-skating in padded bodysuits, my parents absolutely required us to wear close-toed shoes while riding our bikes. To reinforce this rule, Dad told us about his brother who, while riding on the back of my dad's bike when they were kids, failed to wear his shoes. That brother discovered how easily a bike chain could snatch off a toe, especially when it was dangling down, uncovered by a shoe. This rule was later reinforced when my sister decided to break the rule while riding back to our house from the neighborhood swimming pool. She discovered what happens to toenails when unshod feet slip off the pedals and get lodged underneath those pedals at high speeds over asphalt. The memory still solicits a biological reaction in me.

For a man who can't feel his feet, shoes create an unnecessary barrier of insulation to further curb any sensations to the sporadic nerve ending that still fires off something to the brain. The idea is to preserve whatever feeling is still there. To that end, Dad resolved to disobey his own rule, apparently determining that the rule would not apply for scooters as much as it would for bicycles.

Dad purchased the scooter in the spring, giving him plenty of time to learn to ride the thing before the beautiful days of summer hit. So, by June and July, Dad had rediscovered his mobility. No longer bound to the schedules of the city bus or the battery life of his power wheelchair, Dad had begun enjoying the warmth of the sun on his back, the coolness of the wind over his balding head as he throttled those undersized two wheels into a renewed sense of freedom.

The problem with a man riding a scooter with unshod feet in congested city traffic in the middle of summer manifested itself one day when Dad decided to stop for a good serving of wings at KFC. Traffic congestion necessitates frequent stops with only a few feet at a time before having to stop again. In a car, as long as the engine coolant is working, traffic is no big deal. Particularly on a breezy day, most folks just roll down a couple of windows and enjoy the cooling breeze, no shirt or shoes required. But on a scooter, it's a different story.

Imagine the pain my dad did *not* feel every time he stopped in that congested traffic. Every time he waited at a red light. Every time he waited for a pedestrian to cross the street. Sure, all he actually needed to ride the scooter was a butt to sit on and a hand to work the throttle. Stopping was a different story. Feet balance scooters when inertia cannot. Unfortunately, in my dad's case, his feet – covered in a dirty tube sock – couldn't feel anything.

So, it was when Dad walked into KFC that day (encountering looks of horror at the trail of blood that he was leaving behind) that he learned what I learned as a kid at the beach. Asphalt, when in contact with unshod feet for long periods of time, will yield a good, solid third degree burn.

Though I can't say he ever wore shoes again, he certainly learned from the experience. After his feet healed, he added a second layer of tube socks.

# Lay It Down

Most folks remember what it was like to discover the freedom obtained in riding their first bike. My first two-wheeler was the stereotypical, red Schwinn Stingray with coaster brakes and a sweet glittery banana seat. The same thing happens with a first car. Mine was a tan 1968 Volkswagen Beetle. My grandfather passed it down to me, and it was indeed a peach of a ride.

One of the things that I have noticed about people as they age is that they tend to get bigger and bigger cars as they experience new senses of freedom. They trade in sports coups for compact sedans. Compact sedans become mid-size sedans/minivans/SUVs. Mid-size automobiles become full-size until finally, if one lives long enough and keeps his license long enough, that person eventually finds himself behind the wheel of a government-issued, armored tank that gives him the freedom to run through brick walls without being harmed. I remember when my grandfather went from that 1968 VW Beetle he eventually gave me to a 1973 Ford LTD. That was a huge jump. From compact sedan to tank.

My father did the same until he began to regress. I remember his Karmann Ghia, his Vette, VW Rabbit, the Mercedes 280 D, 300 E, and the 560 SEL. That was a normal progression, I guess – at least in terms of size.

Then came the quick regression:

The Mercedes 240 D.

Then the Scooter.

Yeah, that's right, a scooter. It was a blue and silver no-name DUI bike – a high-pitched slug among centipedes whining down the highway near the emergency lane. At least it didn't have pedals. My dad had long-since lost his license, and for a man who needs mobility and wants to see his grandchildren, it was his only answer to his dilemma. By the time Dad found his way to the scooter, I was living in the mountains with my wife and daughter; and Dad had become a grandfather four times over.

Needing to scratch the itch to see his youngest granddaughter, Dad was on his way for a visit when the phone rang.

"Hello?" I spoke into the phone, not recognizing the number.

"Hello. Is this Jonathan?"

"Yes."

"Sir, I don't want to alarm you, but I am with your father. He has had an accident, and he'd like to speak with you. Okay?"

That was how this particular visit with my father had begun – with a mysterious call from a stranger at the site of an accident.

The day had begun as a brisk one for Dad, and as the normal 2-hour-trip-by-car had turned into the 4-hour-trip-by-scooter, Dad was making his way from his home in Charlotte to my home in Boone. The first four hours of the trip had been uneventful. He had made his periodic stops to go to the bathroom, drink some water, and rest. But climbing the mountain up HWY 321, just before the last curve as you enter Watauga County and Blowing Rock, Dad's body collapsed with exhaustion. He laid it down. Right in the middle of traffic, he laid it down. Climbing a two-lane, mountian road, congested with road construction, he laid down the blue and silver high-pitched slug of a DUI bike. Isn't that traumatic enough?

Now picture a 300-pound man laying down a scooter in heavy traffic.

Wearing a bicycle helmet.

A backwards bicycle helmet.

And no shoes.

The diabetic issues had continued to increase the loss of feeling in his feet. After the third-degree burns, I thought he'd return to being part of the shod world, at least while riding the scooter. But he truly didn't care. I understood the extent of his anesthesia when I saw how he cut his toenails.

For years he had struggled to cut his toenails because of the way his toe fungus had damaged his toenails; but as he lost the ability to feel his feet, he realized he could change his approach. Specifically, he could go several months without having to cut his toenails at all by simply pulling each one out with a pair of pliers. Of course they still bled everywhere, but, as an extra perk, it was a surefire way of keeping his neighbors from helping themselves to his coffee. People don't like to visit when you're bleeding all over the furniture. When someone can regularly use a torture method on himself without any pain whatsoever, all for the sake of convenience, there are greater problems than the loss of feeling. Toenails or no toenails, he could barely walk. It's really hard to balance with no feeling in your feet.

So when that woman called me and told me there had been an accident and put him on the phone, I had no idea what I was about to hear.

"I'm below Blowing Rock. I laid the bike down. They want you to come get me."

Dad had begun calling the scooter his "bike"…kind of like a Harley.

I thought it was interesting. *They* wanted me to come get him. Did that mean *he* did not want me to come get him? Experience told me that it was always a good idea to try to understand Dad's circumstances before I entered them – sort of like finding out what's going to happen in a root canal treatment before the procedure actually begins. As I considered the information I had so far, I decided it couldn't be too bad. Otherwise, he would have been in an ambulance.

Knowing I needed a way to transport Dad's wrecked scooter, I called a friend with a big pickup truck. He had heard some of my stories about Dad, and he knew some of what we might be getting into. Granted, I wasn't exactly sure of where Dad was; but when I thought about the curvy mountain road, the stopped traffic, the police car's flashing lights, the crashed scooter, and the shoeless fat man with a backward bicycle helmet, I figured the scene would be pretty easy to spot.

When I arrived, the woman on the phone was gone. It was just Dad, the "bike," and the State Trooper. The Trooper was concerned for Dad. I understood why. We all were.

It seemed odd talking to the State Trooper as he pointed out all of the very obvious dangers about this situation.

*(Does this guy really think he's telling us something we haven't considered?)*

It dawned on me that the Trooper thought we had some sort of control over Dad.

*(He obviously doesn't know anything about my father's refusal to obey anything resembling a rule.)*

When Dad stood up and began to make his way to the truck, the Trooper's face changed.

*(Ahh, he hadn't seen Dad try to walk yet!)*

When he stumbled, the Trooper jumped up quickly to catch him. The Trooper must have realized the ridiculousness of the whole scene in that moment because he quit making suggestions for Dad's care, got back in the car, and left the scene.

We loaded the scooter – scraped and with a dangling mirror – into the back of the truck, hoisted Dad into the cab, and made the last little bit of Dad's journey with him. I rode the scooter in our neighborhood once we arrived to see if it still ran. It was fine other than that dangling mirror. His possessions had increasingly begun to reflect the state of their owner.

Three days later he made the trip home in four hours flat. My guess is that Trooper spent more time figuring out what to put in his report than Dad spent entertaining any suggestion to quit riding the bike, dangling mirror and all.

# **Impacted**

Many things intensify with age.

Cheese.
Fear.
Dirty diapers.
Scotch.
Wrinkles.
Trash.
Responsibilities.
Gray hair.
Wine.
Political opinions.
Dementia.
Fish bait.
Mold.
Knee pain.
Regrets.
Toe fungus.
Debt.
Wisdom.
Antiques.
Infection.
Mean people – yes, the characteristics of people often intensify as well. That was certainly the case with Dad.

My dad was always a little on the messy side. Actually, he was a little on the gross side. Sometimes it was frustrating, like when he cooked breakfast. It was always an event – a feast. It was never a bowl of cereal. When Dad cooked, it was pancakes, eggs, sausage, bacon, biscuits, livermush, and toast – the works. He used the entire kitchen as his prep station. The result could be flour on the counters, jelly on the ceiling, or maybe an egg stuck to the window. Food splattered everywhere.

Sometimes he was just disgusting. He would lie on the couch, raise his leg, and rip the biggest farts ever heard. The floor vibrated. And the smell was horrendous. It would take a while for the funk to disperse – possibly so long that his victims might think they had been spared. And then the stench of rotting sulfuric corpses would invade the nasal passages, causing an instinctive switch to open-mouth breathing that resulted in gagging on the lingering taste in the air. It was putrid.

He used to blow his nose a lot because of the cocaine. But he didn't use a tissue or napkin or handkerchief. He was a snot-rocket kind of man. He used to roll up to stop lights, open the door of the car, lean out with his finger holding one side of his nose, and forcefully blow out the contents of his sinus cavity into the road. It happened all the time. A short, powerful burst of air forced out of his nose with a horrible spray of nose hair and mucus.

One of the grossest times I remember was the morning I walked into my parents' bedroom while Dad was in bed. I was innocent and unsuspecting. I was just going in there to ask a question. Although it was mid morning, Dad was still sleeping in. Mom was already up and had certainly prepared a wonderful, nutritious breakfast for me – a sweet child who was kind-hearted; compassionate; and a completely selfless angel. I began to ask my dad a question, but I didn't even have time to get the question out before it happened.

I heard it. The massive exhale – like the high-pressure release of an air compressor. So. Very. Much. Force.

I felt it. Then I saw it. It was that order. The memory is vivid.

Hear. Feel. See.

I felt it hit my hand. And there in the palm of my hand was the most gargantuan, nasty, green-gray booger I have ever seen in my entire life. I heaved as I ran to the sink.

His grossness got worse with age.

After we had all moved out and Dad was living on his own, we didn't really know how vile he had allowed his living conditions to get until we had to relocate him. We moved him several times because Dad had a really hard time living with rules. He lived in many places because he got kicked out of many places.

Our family only occupied two houses during my entire childhood and adolescence. Once my parents split, however, Dad drifted from place to place:

His mother's downstairs apartment: He was asked to leave because he couldn't get along with the family.

His apartment just down the street from my college: He evacuated because the landlord was the D.A. and Dad had a warrant for failure to appear in court on fourteen different speeding tickets and driving while his license was revoked.

A Condo at Myrtle Beach. He had to leave because he was trying to live "under the radar," secretly sneaking in and out of the condo until the owners discovered him.

His car: It was impounded when the police found drug paraphernalia in it.

The Homeless Shelter: He moved on because he got into an assistance program.

His first apartment in Charlotte: He got back on drugs and overdosed, causing him to lose the apartment and have to go back into treatment.

An assisted living facility that we eventually just called "The Manor": He thought it was too much money so he simply quit paying them.

A retirement facility: He was evicted because he kept running his power wheelchair through the walls in the hallway…among other things.

His second apartment: He was evicted because he thought he shouldn't have to pay rent when he was taken to the hospital for an impacted colon.

The list goes on for nearly a decade longer during which time he was eventually kicked out of a rest home/funeral home combo and had to leave Charlotte because there were no other places that would take him. But it was the last place in the above list, that second apartment, where I was truly horrified. I had helped

Dad find the apartment. It was in a pretty good location. It was on the first floor and close to the bus stop and his bank. It had one bedroom with a good-sized living room, kitchen, bathroom, and eating area – everything one would expect and much nicer than most of the places that had kicked him out. He had been so particular in picking out the apartment, and he finally settled on this one. We moved his belongings from the retirement facility to the new apartment, and everything worked out until his medication got out of whack. Then he got sick and went into the hospital with an impacted colon. I don't really know what that is, but it was a regular occurrence with Dad. It doesn't make sense to me based on what I saw in that apartment. "Impacted" would seem to allude to a lack of movement. And that, dear reader, is not the evidence I found in that apartment.

I got the call that Dad was in the hospital just as he was being released to another dumpy facility. Dad said that he was being evicted and asked me to go get his things again. I rented a truck, and one of my friends who worked with NGOs in third world countries agreed to drive down and pack it up with me. I'm glad he had experience in bad, contaminated situations.

We walked in and looked around. The smell distracted us from the mess. Much of the scene was what one might expect from my dad. Repulsive dishes that hadn't been cleaned in weeks sat in the sink, on the counter, and scattered all over the place. Mounds of cigarettes filled makeshift ashtrays on tables and on the floor. Mysterious stains lived on cushions and countertops. But where it was truly ghastly was in his bedroom. And did I mention the smell? The pungent, acidic smell that lingered everywhere?

We had begun loading things into the truck. We were wearing gloves – gloves we knew we would throw away. The sofa was packed. The kitchen table was packed. The chairs were packed. Everything except the bedroom. We had to get that bed. But there were some things in the way. So we started moving them. We weren't really looking at the items we moved. It was just about clearing space to get that bed out of there. My friend grabbed a vacuum. I grabbed a duffel bag. He moved a stool. I grabbed the trashcan.

A kitchen trashcan.

A blue trashcan.

A heavy trashcan.

Suspiciously, I looked inside.

It was filled about three-fourths of the way.

With vomit.

I still remember how it sloshed up the sides when I moved it. I put my hand over my mouth and ran outside. I had found the source of the smell. It had been there for at least a week. It was unnatural.

All I could think of was if it splashed up on me.

What if I accidentally knocked it over?

What if it leaked?

I know that there are some people who have strong stomachs:

People who clean public restrooms.
Those wonderful folks who put our trash in the big trucks.
People who bus tables in restaurants.

But me, a person who can accidentally touch a slug and gag? I think that booger scarred me. It doesn't take much to make me heave. So a big, blue, kitchen trashcan full of week-old, sloshing vomit? Yeah, that was a problem.

We decided to set the trashcan aside.

My friend ripped the sheets off the bed while I moved the puke can. He threw the sheets away, and we grabbed the mattress. It was muscle memory as we lifted it. We didn't think about it. We just lifted it. Onto its side, we lifted it. I had one hand under it and one hand on its side to steady it. It started to tilt toward me. I braced it with my face.

With my face.

Naturally, I closed my eyes. When the mattress was stabilized, I opened them. On one hand, I'm sorry I opened them. On the other, I'm glad I only opened my eyes…and not my mouth.

Because what was on that mattress right there in front of my eyes (and inches away from my nose) was the very thing that gives me pause when I'm told he was in the hospital for an impacted colon. It appeared that things had been moving along with no obstruction whatsoever. It smelled like it too.

I dropped that mattress. And I washed my face.

I'll take a booger on the hand any day.

# Collateral Damage

My grandmother was dying, and it had been about five years since my father had seen her. Given the fact that Dad could no longer feel his feet, he could no longer drive, even on an illegal basis. And since someone had stolen his scooter, he had become dependent upon family or Greyhound for his long-distance transportation. My sister and I agreed that we needed to take my dad to see his mother. Because nothing was ever simple with my dad, we developed a plan. My sister and I were to meet in Gastonia in the mall parking lot around 10:30 AM. Since I was going to drive my wife's Toyota Corolla and my sister drove a Suburban, we were going to leave her bus in the lot in favor of the better gas mileage offered by the close-quartered, compact sedan. We were going a half-hour down the road to pick up Dad together in Charlotte, take him a little over two hours to the Sanford hospital to see his mother, and return him four hours later to his place in Charlotte – all planning to be back in Gastonia by 5:00 to meet my sister's family for dinner.

Everything was going great. My sister and I had successfully met and begun our journey in the Corolla. We were running early, so we called Dad to let him know. It was best not to have to spend more time than needed at Dad's place. It was a cesspool.

We found Dad waiting for us at the far end of the parking lot. He was wearing sweatpants and sitting in his power wheelchair. *Check. He was wearing pants. We were still in the zone.* We pulled up and opened the door. My sister tends to get car sick, so she was hoping to ride shotgun. I was concerned about this because my dad was still a large man. True, his weight roller-coastered a good bit, but he managed to keep it between a "healthy" 280 and 320. Whether he was going to fit in the back seat of the Corolla or not, I was a little iffy; but when we opened the door, that's when I noticed the feet.

My dad's feet were gross. Always. For as long as I can remember, his feet grossed me out. But after about his fifth life, it got worse. The diabetes created a nightmarish image that could be featured in a John Carpenter film. He couldn't feel his feet. So when he arbitrarily ran over them in his wheelchair, he had no idea. Skin broke. Blood oozed. Bone showed. And he was always clueless to this. To make matters worse, they couldn't heal. They got infected, and he ended up losing toes. It's not like they fell off. It never went that far. But he'd had a couple of them amputated, and he'd lost a section of one foot to the knife as well.

On this fantastically cool day, Dad was wearing a sock on his unshod left foot – one of those hospital gripper-socks. On his right foot, however, dad wore a bandage covered by one of those surgical shoe covers. The thought of what might be under that bandage triggered my gag reflex. Especially when I watched him basically fold his foot in half to force it under the front seat as we stuffed the rest of his body into the back seat. But once he was in, that was it. My sister and I took the front seats, and off we went. As we drove away, we looked at each other, marveling at the lack of Dad's stench that usually reeked of urine and cigarettes. Things were going well.

We stopped for lunch. The question went through my mind as dad said he was hungry. *Where are we going? McDonald's? Arby's? Burger King? Wendy's? KFC? Oh God, please not Taco Bell. And that's when I found out that my fears were too narrowly focused. Fast-food choices were not the least of my problems. Dad picked Chili's – a sit-down restaurant. A new host of questions came to my mind: How will we get him inside? What if he has to go to the bathroom? Will people leave because of us?*

We turned into the lot, pulled up close to the door, and retrieved the walker from the trunk. That's when I realized that those new questions didn't even cut it. He pulled that foot out from under the seat, stood up behind the walker, and began to shuffle to the door. I threw up a little in my mouth when I saw the foot. He was bleeding through the bandage and shoe cover.

Fast-forward through the meal that we shared. I say "shared" intentionally here because he shared his meal with us all. Turns out that one of the things teeth do is keep the food in our mouths when we break the rules of etiquette and talk with our mouths full. And, Dad had no teeth. Let's just say it was a shower of sorts. I didn't have much of an appetite.

As we walked him outside, I noticed the foot again. Yes, it was getting worse. When we prepared to stuff him back into the backseat, I noticed another developing problem. The surgical shoe cover that he wore over his bandage was coming off, leaving the heel exposed. I'm no prophet, but I could see the peril before us.

Again, we packed him up and took our places in the front of the car, and headed for the hospital to see my grandmother. My sister and I, during this second leg of the trip with Dad, had begun to notice that familiar funk in the car. The smell, it seemed, could only be produced by my father. It wasn't the superficial stench of cigarettes and urine that we had expected; it was something that smelled somehow much deeper than that. And, it wasn't like it was permeating the entire car, but we could smell something really pungent beginning to emerge.

When we pulled into the parking lot one hour later, we knew he couldn't walk across the lot, so we pulled up to the door to get him a wheelchair. My sister got him out of the car and put him in the chair; I could only notice one thing in that moment. When dad pulled that foot out from under the front seat, there was something that did not come out with him. When I put him in the car at Chili's, it was there. When my sister took him out, it wasn't. The shoe cover was missing. And there was only one place it could be. I parked the car. I walked around to the back seat. I pulled out my phone to illuminate the dark cavern under the seat. I grabbed a napkin from the front seat because I could see what was coming, and I wasn't about to do it bare-handed. I spotted the grotesque, blood-and-disease-infested, makeshift shoe. I reached in and pulled it out. And yes, I gagged. No, I heaved. By this time, I was getting tired of tasting stomach acid. My mind was taking a quick inventory of the plethora of medical issues he faced, and Dad had MRSA. I never totally understood the disease, but here's enough info to give you the picture: It's transferred in body fluids; it's highly contagious; it's life-threatening; and it's incurable. I tossed the MRSA shoe in the trash in the parking lot, but I noticed something else. The smell in the car was gone. Usually the smell that accompanied dad lingered in whatever he was sitting on well after he was gone. It was not the case here. I knew that meant something, but I didn't know what. I should have known.

*****

I walked into the hospital to find my grandmother. I assumed that my sister and my dad would have already arrived in her room, given the extra time I spent parking the car and taking care of the little recon mission under the seat. Alas, I was wrong. Aunts and uncles were there. My grandmother was there. But Dad was nowhere to be found. The fact that my sister was absent from the scene made me feel a little better about it since the chances of any blatant illegal activity were far diminished by her presence.

It wasn't long before my sister wheeled Dad in through the door. It turns out that she had run him by the ER to get something to cover that bleeding foot that had shed it's only barrier to contamination-city. He had what could basically be described as a diaper wrapped around it. There was no evidence of a professional dressing. This was a rigged-up field dressing, a mere second barrier to what could result in a widespread MRSA outbreak.

Dad came in and visited with his mother. It was short. They didn't say too much. But after maybe thirty minutes had passed, the nurse walked in. My sister is a pretty assertive person, and she did not hesitate to ask the nurse for a little favor: "Would you mind taking a look at my Dad's foot and putting a new dressing on it?' The nurse was kind. She said that she would be happy to. I had no idea what motivated her to make the decision to become a nurse, but when she opened up that bandage, she must have been asking some internal questions:

*What did I do to deserve this?*
*Isn't working in retail better than this?*
*How bad is it to vomit in an open wound?*

I felt pretty sure that she, at the very least, would never agree to help someone like this again with such graciousness. People like my dad are the reason some nurses decide they hate their jobs.

She knelt down in front of my dad on the other side of my grandmother's hospital bed. Thankfully, the scene took place outside my line of sight. After a moment, I simply heard her say, "Ohhhhh," in a way that let me know something was wrong. And if that wasn't enough to clue me in, the return of the smell I had noticed in the car should have been. It filled the room. But it wasn't a mysterious smell anymore. It was distinctively like the smell of roadkill, and it filled the room the same way the smell of a skunk does when hit by a car. Once again, I found myself trying to hold down my lunch. The nurse said it again: "Ohhhhh." But this time "Ohhhhh" was followed by, "Nooooo." She was obviously disturbed.

"Has a doctor seen this?" she asked.

"Yesterday," my dad replied.

"Because this is bad. It's a diabetic ulcer."

"I know," he said. "It's been there like that for a couple months."

"I can see about two inches of the bone in your foot."

And that's when I thanked God that I was on the other side of the bed. Sometimes obstructions are good – very good.

"Well, I'm going to redress this," she continued, "but you need to get this checked out. It's really bad."

In my mind, when I hear a medical professional say that something is bad, it's kind of like Eric Clapton saying you're the best guitarist he's ever heard. Either it's simply untrue, or it's a very big deal. But Dad's thinking was different. As a matter of fact, he expressed his own sense of urgency by asking if we could visit the Chic-Fil-A for a sandwich before we left the hospital. I still don't know why they have a Chic-Fil-A in the hospital in Sanford. I guess it goes back to the days when Chic-Fil-A was only in malls. And maybe since Sanford didn't have a mall, the next most logical place was the hospital.

So we took Dad and his freshly bandaged skunk foot down to the Chic-Fil-A. "What do you want, Dad?" I asked.

"I just want one of those chicken sandwiches…and a lemonade."

We wheeled him over toward a table.

"Don't you want anything?" he asked.

Honestly, for a split second, I thought about it. Lunch at Chili's had been pretty skimpy as I tried to get it down during the food shower. I was a little hungry. But then I looked down at that foot. That's the first time I had looked at it since the nurse had redressed it. Bad mistake. When she wrapped it, she did so correctly…

from a medical perspective. But from an aesthetic perspective? From an I'd-like-to-eat-a-chicken-sandwich perspective? Not so much. She left the toes uncovered. They weren't bleeding. At least for the moment. She had merely covered the wound. Which is technically what a bandage is supposed to do. The problem is that, like I said before, Dad's feet were gross without having a gaping open diabetic ulcer.

Flashback: One of my childhood friends had a pet goat…until his family decided to eat it. Seeing that goat prepared on the table had bothered me. But the worse part was when my friend took me in the backyard to see the goat's guts they had tossed in the trashcan. I don't remember much of what I saw. But I remember the stomach. It was swollen and gray. We poked it with a stick, and it was kind of rubbery – like one of those cheap balls you see in the bins in discount stores.

That's what came to mind when I looked down and saw Dad's foot.

Gray.

Swollen.

Rubbery.

The foot looked especially disturbing when he ran it into one of the table legs and I just watched it sort of flop to the side. The worst part, I think, was the jacked up toenails sticking straight out. Swollen toes with these jagged bloodstained, yellowish-brown, fungus-infested toenails. They almost looked like rotten wood.

And that's when I knew there was no way I was eating a chicken sandwich in the hospital Chic-Fil-A that day. And that's when I was ready to get Dad in the car and put this day behind me.

*****

We wheeled Dad out to the car. We got him back into the backseat, and I took notice of the goat-stomach, skunk foot disappearing under the front seat again – back home in its cave. My sister and I got back in the front seat of the Corolla and pointed it back toward Charlotte. With any luck, we only had two more hours of this trip from Hell, and we were ready to get home.

We all made small talk for about 55 minutes while Dad dozed in and out behind my sister. Everything was going fine. Things were finally starting to look normal. That is, normal for a MRSA-infested, swollen gray, oozing foot suffering from near-gangrene, diabetic ulcers riding under the front seat. And it was then, at the pinnacle of the trip, when my hopes were at their highest for an uneventful conclusion to the trip that my Dad spoke up: "I'm going to need you to find a bathroom."

Coincidentally, we were pulling into another town when he requested this, so things were still looking good.

"No problem, Dad. We should be able to find one right up here."

I approached the first stoplight and pulled into a shopping center on the right. He was going to have trouble making it with his walker to a bathroom in the rear of a store, so I was looking for a store likely to have a bathroom at the front. As I was cruising past these stores, a gas station across the street caught my eye. Bathrooms in gas stations never require a long walk. I turned the car toward the gas station. That's where we were heading when I drove across the road, pulled into the parking lot, and heard the most disturbing thing I have ever heard.

My father grunted, "Humphhh. Damn."

Complete horror swelled within me. I looked at my sister. Since I could see the whites of her eyes, I knew she feared the same thing I did; but I said nothing since all I could do was focus on getting to the door. I pulled the car right next to the side door and slid it into park. And that's when I heard it again: "Humphhh. Damn."

I popped the trunk, jumped out of the car, grabbed the walker, and opened Dad's door. His response to my haste? "Hurry," he groaned.

As I helped him out of the car, I dared to ask the question we all knew the answer to. "Dad, did you just have a blow out in my car?"

Again under a guttural groan of haste and discomfort, he moaned, "Hurry."

I helped him out of the car and to his walker, not daring to think about his pants. I was in such a hurry that I didn't even take notice of the foot. As I steadied him shuffling to the door, my sister watched as what had once been inside my dad's bowels made its way down his pant legs. Strangely enough, in that moment, it didn't even cross my mind that a man emptying his bowels while walking on a swollen, gray, almost-dead MRSA foot behind a walker into a gas station was abnormal. I was completely motivated by fear. Adrenaline began to rush through my body. I opened the door to the gas station, but I apparently wasn't fast enough as Dad repeatedly bumped his walker into the door. There was no time for patience. Cataclysmic disaster was upon us.

"Where's the bathroom?" he half-moaned, half-barked at the gas station attendants as he shuffled across the tile with the foot dragging about six inches at a time.

Following the attendants' directions, we rounded the corner. Last door on the left. We made it. I grabbed the handle and opened the door.

I'm still not sure how it happened, but somehow I found myself in the bathroom with him. Cornered, I was between him and the toilet. He was between the door and me. We both blocked each other's paths. That's when I found myself in the most perilous situation of the entire day because in that moment, in that half-groan/half-bark, my father uttered these words in complete urgency: "Help me."

No one wants to do that.

He was already pulling off his jacket. He couldn't get it by himself. I helped him pull it off. He unbuttoned his pants with one hand while hanging on to the walker with the other. His pants slid to the floor and he fell onto the toilet.

As he fell onto the toilet, I noticed his shirttail still wrapped under his butt cheeks. Just in time, I grabbed the back of his shirt, pulling it out of the danger zone. And that's when I saw what no son should ever have to see. The thing that brings flashbacks and causes me to shudder with disgust. I saw it fall out of him. Right there. Mid-air. I saw the bombs begin to drop.

I slapped my hand over my mouth, not sure if I was keeping my vomit in or his fumes out, and ran for the door.

As the door closed behind me, the war zone took on additional fire. I was safe. Or, so I thought.

I stood there in the hall hoping and praying. *Please, God, don't let anyone come around that corner.*

As I uttered these primal, instinctive prayers, I couldn't help but hear the noises on the other side of the door. I had seen it in movies, but I had never experienced it in real life until that moment. He was moaning. Audibly. Loudly.

Something horrific was taking place behind that door.

My sister rounded the corner in an attempt to check on things. She had come in to purchase something to mask the smell in the car. When she rounded the corner, she stopped dead in her tracks. Her face turned white. And she hurriedly went back the way she came.

What stopped her short of the end of the hall was the smell. It had hit her in the face like a huge boxing glove. The air completely evacuated her lungs the same it does when you fall three feet flat on your back on the playground as a kid.

I smelled it too. I just didn't think it had made it that far down the hall.

She sent me a text: "The smell is coming around the corner."

I let her know how much worse it was at my end of the hall with my quick response: "I'm gagging."

A few minutes later, I heard a bump on the door. It startled me, but when he called out my name I felt the blood drain from my body. I gripped the door handle and opened Pandora's Box. I thought Dad had suddenly gained a new appreciation for cleanliness; he was washing his hands at the sink. Maybe this wasn't going to be so bad. But right in the middle of that thought, I noticed the curious wad of toilet paper under the sink. As I tried to determine where the toilet paper had come from and how it had gotten there, I noticed something even more curious. Most of it was brown. And then it got worse. I was reminded of the cats our family had when I was a child: One of the things that always perplexed me about cats is the way they dig a whole, drop a load, and only partially cover it up. There's always that little bit just peeking out, saying, "Here I am; don't forget about me." Well, it turns out that Dad had a lot in common with those cats because what was under that brown wad of toilet paper was his own little peek-er. It was screaming, "Don't forget about me; I'm here, right under this wad of brown toilet paper." And there he was, washing his hands over the peek-a-boo poop. The smell was horrendous. The sight was ghastly. How did it get there? And that's when I took the survey of the rest of the room. I've seen those movies where planes come in and bomb targets – big targets – over and over again. It leaves these burnt holes everywhere one of those bombs lands – like a huge divot or crater. That was the bathroom. All over the floor were the places where my father had apparently bombed. There were uncovered piles everywhere. It was like Dad had mutated from cat to dog. *Cover it. Nah, just leave it.* It was everywhere. Piles of the stuff that gave off a toxicity equivalent to that of Chernobyl. My dad had dropped atomic bombs all over the bathroom.

My mouth dropped open in horror. I quickly closed it. That's not an environment where you want to have your mouth open.

The bomber spoke. "We gotta go."

"What happened?" I pleaded.

"I had to go." That was his explanation.

"Dad," I marveled, "When I left you in here, your butt was on the toilet, and this was not here. How did this happen?"

In my mind, it was impossible. The floor was clean when he entered. He sat on the toilet. And suddenly random piles of feces were all over the room? That can't happen. Not when he is the only person in the room.

Again, his only reply: "I had to go."

"Dad," I said, "There have been lots of times I've had to go." And pointing at the piles, "But I've never done THAT."

"I had to go," he repeated.

And what he did after that was the worst thing imaginable. He stepped back. And I watched one of those piles squish beneath that MRSA-infested, near-gangrene, diabetic-ulcer-ed, gray skunk-foot. I swear I could almost hear it. And then he took another step back with the gripper sock into another pile.

He shoved the walker between the door and the doorframe. Then out he shuffled into the hall.

Two fecal feet, one socked and one bandaged were laving streaks of brown in his wake. He didn't seem to care, but I felt complete shame as he smeared the remains down the hall.

He staggered through the door of the gas station, opened the car door, and got in. I watched those fecal feet slide across the carpet in the floor of my car, and I couldn't believe this was happening to me. My sister and I got back in the front seat and quickly realized there was absolutely no way this was going to happen without altering the situation. An hour car ride back to his place? The smell was like trying to inhale with dog crap shoved up your nose. Not that I know what that is entirely like, but it must be pretty similar. We did what anyone in a precarious, emergency situation would do. We did what I did when my wife went into labor. We went to Wal-Mart. My sister went in for supplies. I expected carbon-filter masks, hazmat coveralls, and an excavator. What we got was rubber gloves, Clorox wipes, and plastic bags.

The gloves were for her hands. The plastic bags were for his feet. The Clorox wipes were for the brown streaks. I won't take a guess at how many times she heaved, but it was extensive.

We got back in the car and found ourselves gasping for air again. It was 35 degrees outside. The car's heater acted as an oven – an oven baking human dung pies. We had no choice. The windows came down. My head went out the window like I was Ace Ventura, and that's how we made the hour-long trip of hell. Dad complained continuously about being cold. I almost felt sorry for him, but then we would stop at a stop sign; the smell would stop moving, fill up the car again in the stagnant air, and recirculate to slap you in the face like a cinder block – a cinder block filled with steaming cow patties.

We dumped him off at his place, and started taking steps to get the residue out of the car. Our plan involved a rented steam cleaner, a car wash, new floor mats, and pet spray. The plan didn't work as well as we had hoped, and I found myself making the two-hour drive back to my house in what amounted to a MRSA-mobile. By morning, my entire garage smelled like that gas station bathroom.

He never rode in my car again. Hazmat ended up coming to the house and setting up a little ET scene right in our driveway to tear out the interior of the car and burn it. The body shop installed new carpet and seats. The total damage done to the Corolla was just over $7,000. But it's no big deal.

He had to go.

# Conclusion: Dust and Bones

Saturday, January 26, 2013, was an overcast day with a little breeze in the winter air. Two cars pulled into the public parking area of a fishing pier at a North Carolina beach. There were nine of us – ten of us, if you count Dad. He was in the trunk. And, even though Dad was riding alone in the trunk, this strange trip was all about him.

We had picked Dad up a week earlier at a funeral home/crematory we found on the Internet. We chose it because of the cost, thinking there couldn't be much difference in funeral homes, especially when it comes to a basic cremation.

The place looked nice enough to us when we parked in the storefront parking lot and walked down the alley to the entrance. It had a faux comfort aesthetic, kind of like listening to a sleek salesman push a budget timeshare in Branson. One of the directors greeted us and escorted us to a conference table where we made decisions surrounded by urns and signed enough paperwork to warrant a real estate investment. She dignified my father's death by being direct. She used words like "purge" and "condition of the body." Kind but assertive, she was dressed in a tasteful black polyester pantsuit with a blood-red blouse and black loafers.

We returned a week later to pick him up. Dad was in a gift bag when the director handed him to me. He was surprisingly heavy. It didn't have a bow, but I appreciated the convenient handle. Inside that gift bag, his remains were in two bags – a little one and a larger one – both tucked inside a plastic box. The remains were separated like that in order for us to honor Dad's wishes –

the wishes that took us to the beach that overcast day at the end of January.

Dad had grown up at the beach. A god in the water, Dad used to jump off the end of one fishing pier and swim in the ocean current a couple miles down to the next fishing pier. Eventually, he got a job working as a lifeguard there and was able to save many a drowning beach-goer before the days of rescue tubes and ATVs. Poseidon had nothing on Dad. This fishing pier was a second home for him during the glory days of his adolescence and young adulthood. His sustenance came from hot dogs on the pier and beer from the bars surrounding it. With his fondness for this particular pier, long since rebuilt from the ruins left by several hurricane assaults, Dad had requested his ashes be spread into these waters from this nostalgic pier. It would have been a nice gesture if it weren't illegal.

We had a foolproof plan and considered everything imaginable. We had even divided Dad from two bags into three smaller bags. Dad's brothers and sisters wanted some of him to bury in a grave plot. We wanted to honor their request, and so the ash-division was a task my wife graciously accepted. It was a final bonding moment for her and Dad. When she opened the large bag, she pondered the physics of moving an ashy, dusty, crumbly substance from one open bag to a Ziploc storage bag. It turns out that one of the corners "budget crematoriums" cut is in the plastic bag department. Barely noticeable to the naked eye, there was a hole. And, when she began the process of displacing half of Dad's ashes to the Ziploc, Dad made his final move. She plopped the bag down and it became an atomic bomb, it's gray mushroom cloud filling the air above…surrounding her. By instinct she shut her eyes and squeezed her lids tight. All she could think about in those few seconds was the array of medical conditions that plagued Dad (See Supplemental Interlude for a full listing).

*Which ones were contagious?*
*Was that fire in the crematorium hot enough to kill everything?*

The cloud swam around her. She gasped in horror. And, yes, she breathed him in. Like a deep draw of air when you come up from swimming underwater, she breathed him in. He filled her nasal passages. He filled her sinuses. He filled her lungs. Like an unexpected puff of second-hand smoke, he swirled through her. Out of shock, she opened her mouth. He stuck to her tongue like chalk. Dust particles settled on her teeth. She left what she was doing and brushed her teeth. And flushed her sinuses with saline. And took a shower. It had been their last moment together.

She finished the task and handed him to us graciously in three bags. It was the smallest of the bags that we pulled out of the trunk. We had arrived in the morning before the temperature rose to tolerance. We were maneuvering so as not to get caught, Dad tucked safely in my jacket pocket, just along for one last illegal ride. We climbed the stairs to the pier, remembering the days we played in the sand below. Remembering the rush of riding waves as he taught us to body surf. Remembering his big, hairy body sprawled out baking beneath the hot, summer sun. Remembering the beach houses he had rented when we were kids. Remembering the Birdwell swim trunks he had insisted on buying me each year at the beach. Remembering the only sin at the beach had been to wear socks.

We each paid our dollar to access the fishing pier. *We're just tourists having a look around.*

And that is precisely when we discovered that our plan was flawed. We hadn't thought about the possibility of fishing tournaments in winter. Sure enough, the big winter tournament had just started. We stepped onto the pier, looking for an inconspicuous place to dump Dad and hold an impromptu, illegal memorial service. The tournament was going on all day, so it was our only chance at this. We had to seize the moment. It was all he had asked of us. We walked to the end of the pier. Nonchalantly, we wandered around, standing awkwardly between groups of fishermen. *No, we don't have rods or coolers. We are just part of the regular fan base that makes fishing a spectator sport!*

I'm not absolutely certain we stood out, considering that we were the only people on the pier who weren't fishing, who were not dressed for the occasion, who had actually paid a dollar to just walk out there, and who were carrying the ashes of a dead man in their pockets. Other than that, we were completely incognito.

The end of the pier was no good. It was crowded. We were sure to be spotted. So we began the walk back to the beach-end of the pier where the gift shop, bait shop, and grill were. About halfway down the pier we stopped. There was a gap of about 15 feet between two fishermen. Most of the ones around were rifling through the beer, bait and fish in their coolers; we decided this was it. It was now or never. We all gathered in a cluster at the rail, and everyone leaned over as I reached in my pocket for the baggie. Under the cover of the cluster, I knelt down, opened the baggie, and extended my hand through the rail. "Here we go," I eloquently announced as I tipped the baggie. And just as I did, a big ocean breeze swirled around us and billowed Dad out before everyone present. He was a cloud floating on the wind, beautifully irreverent and admittedly illegal. And as Dad descended down into the waters that marked his adolescent playground, the sun came out, breaking through the clouds. The angry, green-brown waves of the Atlantic calmed and turned into a serene blue-green. And we knew that, in our last illegal effort to honor him, he was pleased.

Rest well, Dad.

## About The Author

Jonathan Yarboro learned to tell stories while lying in bed in his underwear, listening to his grandfather tell Wild Bill Hickok stories at bedtime. Though he rarely tells stories in his underwear now, he makes no such claim about his writing. His first short story, though it wasn't very good, was published in a collegiate literary magazine called *The Lyricist*. Jonathan earns a living by talking to people about the collegiate world. He lives with his wife Felicia and daughter Katherine in the mountains of North Carolina.

Join the *Two Trashbags* conversation by visiting www.facebook.com/twotrashbags or www.twotrashbags.com. Follow Jonathan on Twitter at @jonathanyarboro.

www.ingramcontent.com/pod-product-compliance
Lightning Source LLC
Chambersburg PA
CBHW060202050426
42446CB00013B/2954